THE
LAWS
of LUCK

THE LAWS of LUCK

The Success System That Never Fails

BRIAN TRACY

MEDIA

MEDIA

Published 2023 by Gildan Media LLC
aka G&D Media
www.GandDmedia.com

Design by Meghan Day Healey of Story Horse, LLC

Library of Congress Cataloging-in-Publication Data is available upon request

ISBN: 978-1-7225-0628-5

10 9 8 7 6 5 4 3 2 1

CONTENTS

The Laws of Luck

Chapter 1

The Law of Cause and Effect

Everything happens for a reason. For every effect in your life, there is a cause or a series of specific measurable, definable, identifiable causes.

The Law of Action and Reaction

For every action, there is an equal and opposite reaction.

The Law of Sowing and Reaping

"Whatsoever a man soweth, that shall he also reap" (Galatians 6:7).

The Law of Probabilities

For every event, there is a probability of that event occurring under certain circumstances.

The Law of Attraction

You are a living magnet. You inevitably attract into your life the people, circumstances, ideas, and resources that are in harmony with your dominant thoughts.

The Law of Belief

Whatever you believe with conviction becomes your reality.

The Law of Mind

A corollary of the law of belief. Thoughts objectify themselves. Your thoughts eventually materialize in the world around you.

The Law of Expectations

Whatever you expect with confidence becomes your own self-fulfilling prophecy. You get not what you want in life, but what you expect.

The Law of Subconscious Activity

Whatever thought or goal you hold in your conscious mind will be accepted by your subconscious mind as a command or instruction.

The Law of Affirmation

Whatever goals you repeat over and over in a positive, personal, present tense way will be accepted by your subconscious mind as commands. The results will then be drawn into your life by the law of attraction.

The Law of Correspondence

Your outer world reflects your inner world; what is going on outside of you is a reflection or manifestation of what is going on inside of you.

The Law of Mental Equivalents

Your main job is to create within yourself the mental equivalent of what you wish to enjoy on the outside. Past or future thoughts do not count. The only thing that makes a difference is the way you think at this very moment.

The Law of Suggestion

Your thoughts set up a force field of attraction that is either bringing you the things you want or the things that you don't want.

The Law of Responsibility

You are 100 percent responsible for yourself, everything you are, and everything you become.

Chapter 2

The Law of Positive Expectations

The more confidently you expect something good to come out of every situation, the more likely it is to occur.

The Law of Futurity

It doesn't matter where you're coming from; all that matters is where you're going.

The Law of Synchronicity

Things happen that have no direct cause and effect relationship. Events are often linked not by causality but by meaning.

The Law of Purpose

The secret of success is constancy of purpose.

The Law of Control

You feel positive about yourself to the degree to which you feel you are in control of your own life. You feel negative about yourself to the degree to which you feel you are controlled by external forces or other people.

The Law of Accident

The opposite of the law of control, it says that failing to plan means planning to fail. Acting aimlessly means living aimlessly.

The Law of Clarity

The clearer you are about what you want, the more rapidly you will attain it.

The Law of Desire

The only limitation on your abilities is how badly you really want something.

The Law of Accelerating Acceleration

Whatever you are moving toward is moving toward you as well: like attracts like.

The Law of Concentration

Whatever you dwell upon grows and increases in your world.

Chapter 3

The Law of the Winning Edge

Small differences in knowledge and ability can lead to enormous differences in results.

The Law of Integrative Complexity

In every group, the individual who can integrate the greatest amount of information will rise and dominate all the others in that group.

The Law of Self-Development

You can learn anything you need to learn to achieve any goal you set for yourself. There are no limitations on what you can accomplish.

The Law of Talents

You will never develop a useful talent or ability without having, sooner or later, an opportunity to apply that talent or ability to some good purpose.

The Law of Variety

Your success will be determined by the quality and quantity of ideas that you can generate to improve your circumstances.

Chapter 4

The Law of Service

Your rewards will always be equal to the value of your service to others. The universe is always in balance: you will always get out what you put in.

The Law of Practice

Whatever you practice over and over again eventually becomes a new habit or skill.

The Law of Incremental Improvement

You get better little by little and bit by bit. Excellence is a long, laborious process of tiny, incremental advances, each one of which may be imperceptible, but accumulatively, they add up to mastery.

The Law of Decision

People are successful because they have made a clear, unequivocal, do-or-die decision to be successful. Unsuccessful people have never made that decision.

The Law of Love

Everything you do in life is either to get love or to compensate for the lack of love. A corollary is that you will only be truly successful and happy when you commit yourself wholeheartedly to doing what you most love to do.

The Law of Improvement

Your life only gets better when you get better.

Chapter 5

The Law of Liking

The more people like you, the more they will be influenced by you and the more they will help you to achieve your goals.

The Law of Self-Esteem

The more you like respect and appreciate yourself, the more you will like, respect, and appreciate others, and the more they will like, respect, and appreciate you.

The Law of Affirmation
Whatever strong, affirmative statements you repeat over and over in your conscious mind will soon be accepted as commands by your subconscious mind.

The Law of Subconscious Activity
Whatever is accepted by your subconscious mind begins to materialize in the world around you.

The Law of Substitution
Your conscious mind can only hold one thought at a time, and you can choose that thought. You can substitute a positive thought for a negative thought anytime you choose.

The Law of Reversibility
Just as feelings generate actions that are consistent with them, actions generate feelings that are consistent with them. You can act your way into feeling the way you want to feel.

The Law of Emotional Reciprocity
When you do and say things that make other people feel good, they will have an unconscious desire to pay you back and make you feel good as well.

Chapter 6
The Law of Relationships
The more people who know you and think of you in a positive way, the more success and opportunity you will have.

The Law of Repulsion

The converse of the law of attraction: you automatically repel people and circumstances that are not in harmony with your dominant thoughts.

The Law of Indirect Effort

You get what you want with other people more often indirectly than directly.

The Law of Giving

The more you give of yourself without expectation of return, the more will come back to you from the most unexpected sources.

The Law of Indirect Effort

Instead of trying to impress the other person, ask questions and be impressed by what he or she says to you.

The Law of Liking

The more a person likes you, the easier it is to influence them.

The Law of Reciprocity

If you do something for another person, the other person will want to do something for you.

Chapter 7

The Law of Abundance

We live in a universe of unlimited abundance. There is plenty for everyone.

The Law of Emulation

You will be successful to the exact degree to which you find out what other successful people do and you do those things over and over.

The Law of Saving

If you save and invest 10 percent of your income over the course of your working lifetime, you will retire a millionaire.

The Law of Accumulation

Money saved and invested with emotions of hope and desire will develop a force field of energy around it and attract more money.

The Law of Opportunity

When you are ready, exactly the right opportunity will appear to you at exactly the right time.

The Law of Investing

You must investigate before you invest. You must spend at least as much time studying the investments as you spend earning the money you invest.

The Law of Conservation

It is not how much money you earn but how much you keep that counts.

Chapter 8

The Law of Concentration

Whatever you dwell upon grows and increases in your life.

The Law of Decision

Any clear, specific decision to do something definite clears your mind and activates your creativity.

The Law of Superconscious Activity

Any thought, plan, goal, or idea that you hold continuously in your conscious mind must be brought into reality by your super-conscious mind.

Chapter 9

The Law of Results

Your rewards will always be equal to the quality, quantity, and timeliness of the results that you accomplish for other people.

The Law of Applied Effort

Any goal, task, or activity is amenable to the sustained effort of hard work.

The Law of Zero-Based Thinking

If there is any activity that, knowing what you know now, you would not have undertaken to begin with, eliminate that activity as soon as possible.

Chapter 10

The Law of Flexibility

You must be clear about your goal, but you must always remain flexible about the way you attain it.

Chapter 11

The Law of Courage

If you move boldly in the direction of your goals, unseen forces will come to your aid.

The Law of Habit

In the absence of a clear decision on your part or some external stimulus, you will keep on acting in the same way indefinitely. Furthermore, whatever you do over and over again becomes a new habit.

The Law of Assumption

Whatever you sincerely desire, act as if it were impossible to fail, and it shall be.

1

The Fundamental Laws of Luck

Everyone wants to be healthier, happier, more prosperous, and more satisfied. Yet only a few are really living happy, fully functioning, self-actualizing lives. Most people have the uneasy feeling that they could be doing far better than they are today—if only they knew how. They are living well below their inborn potentials for success and happiness. They could be far healthier, earn more money, achieve greater success, recognition, and esteem, and enjoy more satisfying lives than they are today.

Personally, I started off with very few advantages. My parents never had any money, and my father was unemployed for long stretches. I failed out of high school and worked as a laborer for many years. When I was twenty-four, I was still drifting. I was broke, unemployed, deeply in debt, with no skills, no education, no powerful friends, and not much of a future, as far as I could see.

Then I began asking, "Why are some people more successful than others? Why do some people have more money, better jobs, happier families, vibrant health, and exciting lives? They drive nicer cars; they wear nicer clothes and live in better homes. They always seem to have money. They go to nice restaurants, they take nice trips, and they have satisfying lives. Why?"

I was told that successful people were just lucky; those who were unsuccessful and unhappy were just victims of bad luck. Did this mean that people who started off from limited backgrounds, worked hard, studied hard, and pulled themselves up into prominence by their own application and effort were merely lucky? Did this mean that people who had come from all over the world with no friends, no language skills, no money, and no opportunities, but who had become successful, were just lucky? It didn't make sense to me.

According to the global bank Credit Suisse, in 2022 there were more than 22 million millionaires in the United States. Many if not most are self-made. In the same year, some 2.5 million new millionaires were made. Were all these people just lucky?

What I learned, and what I'm about to share with you, is the result of more than twenty-five years of study into the thoughts, feelings, actions, behaviors, and decisions of successful people. The bottom line is that luck is predictable. It is not a series of random, haphazard occurrences that one person gets a lot of and another person gets none. In fact, you can have all the luck you want if you do the things that so-called lucky people do.

Luck is predictable. You can have all the luck you want if you do the things that so-called lucky people do.

The Law of Cause and Effect

In the fifth century B.C., a number of Greek philosophers pro-pounded what has come to be the foundation law of Western philosophy and thought. At a time when everyone believed in the gods on Mount Olympus and the causeless, chaotic influences of the elements, these philosophers stated that we live in a world of law, governed by a system of order, whether we understand the principles behind it or not. Today we summarize these principles as the law of cause and effect. We accept it as a part of the world. But in those days, it was a remarkable idea and hotly debated.

The law of cause and effect says that everything happens for a reason: for every effect in your life, there is a cause or a series of specific measurable, definable, identifiable causes. If there's anything you want in life, an effect that you desire, you can find someone else who's achieved the same result. By doing the things they have done, you can eventually enjoy the same results and rewards.

Success is not an accident. It is not a result of good luck versus bad luck. Even if you have not identified how you got from where you were to where you are today, you have taken a series of specific steps that have brought you here. In fact, they could have brought you to no other place.

You are where you are and what you are because of yourself. Your choices and decisions over the years have determined your life at this moment. The wonderful part of this is that at any time, you can start making different choices and taking different steps, and you will inevitably arrive at a different place than where you are today.

America is full of hundreds of thousands of people who have come from difficult backgrounds, with every conceivable type of handicap and liability, but who have gone on to build wonderful lives for themselves. Often people around them ascribe their good fortunes to luck. But if you talk to these people and trace their stories, you will find that luck had nothing to do with their success—and it has nothing to do with yours.

The law of cause and effect cuts in both directions: it also says that if there is an unfortunate effect in your life, such as lack of money, problems in your relationships, or an unsatisfying job or career, you can trace that effect back to the things that you have done to cause it. By removing the causes, you can remove the effects, sometimes overnight. Successful, happy, and prosperous people have discovered the laws that govern our lives and have designed their lives to be in harmony with those laws. As a result, they experience far more joy and satisfaction and accomplish more in a few years than the average person does in a lifetime.

You've heard it said in poker that the winners laugh and tell jokes while the losers say, "Shut up and deal." In the world around you, the winners are busy and working toward achieving their goals, while the average people are putting in as little as they can and hoping that something good will come out of it. Winners ascribe their success to hard work and application. Mediocre people ascribe their failures to bad luck.

Perhaps the most important corollary of the law of cause and effect is this: thoughts are causes, and conditions are effects. Your mind is the most powerful force in your universe. As Ralph Waldo Emerson said, "A man becomes what he thinks about most of the time."

Thoughts are causes, and conditions are effects.

You are where you are and what you are because of your habitual ways of thinking. Your thoughts are creative, and they ultimately create your reality, so if you change your thinking, you change your life. The greatest thinkers of all time, going back to the earliest religions, philosophers, and metaphysical schools, have all emphasized the power of the human mind to shape individual destiny.

The Law of Action and Reaction

Another version of the law of cause and effect is the law of action and reaction, first propounded by Sir Isaac Newton. It states that for every action, there is an equal and opposite reaction. Put another way, actions have consequences. At the beginning, you can decide upon and control a particular action, but once you have launched it, the consequences are often out of your hands. Once you've done or said a particular thing, the consequences take on a power and a force of their own. This is why all successful people tend to be very thoughtful about what they say and do, while unsuccessful people tend to be thoughtless, even careless, about their statements or behaviors.

The key to enjoying more of what people call luck is to engage in more of the actions that are likely to bring about the consequences that you desire. At the same time, you must consciously decide to avoid those actions that will not bring about the consequences you desire or, even worse, will bring about consequences that you don't want. If you're in sales, the actions of prospecting, presenting, following up, and working continually to cultivate leads and referrals will ultimately bring about the consequences of sales success, higher income, personal pride, and greater satisfaction from your career. The more of these actions you engage in, the more pleasurable consequences you'll enjoy. On the other hand, the fewer of these actions you engage in, the less often you'll enjoy those consequences.

Another restatement of the law of cause and effect is the law of sowing and reaping: as the Bible says, "Whatsoever a man soweth, that shall he also reap" (Galatians 6:7). Whatever you put in, you get out. Whatever you are reaping today is a result of what you have sown in the past.

The laws of cause and effect, action and reaction, sowing and reaping, are timeless truths, universal principles that have existed since the beginning of man on this earth. All success, happiness, and high achievement come from organizing your life in conformity with these timeless principles. When you do, you'll achieve satisfaction at levels seldom experienced by the average person, and people will start to call you lucky.

The Law of Probabilities

The law of probabilities is a critical factor in explaining luck. This law says that for every event, there is a probability of that event occurring under certain circumstances. Events happen in your life with a logical, systematic regularity. For example, if you flip a coin, in the long run, it will come down heads 50 percent of the time and tails 50 percent of the time. The probability of a heads or tails is 50 percent, no matter how many times you flip the coin.

You may flip the same coin 5,000 times, and on every flip of the coin the probabilities remain 50 percent heads, 50 percent tails. In order to enjoy more luck, your primary job is to increase the probabilities of success in every area that's important to you.

Throughout this book, I'll be giving you dozens of ways to influence the probabilities of achieving the results you desire in virtually anything that you do. Here's an example. Imagine a person who has had too much to drink, and who can barely stand up, in a dimly lit room, with a dartboard on the wall thirty or forty feet away. This person has an endless supply of darts to throw at the dartboard. He is not clear-eyed or alert and has no experience of dart throwing, but he begins throwing the darts. What are the odds that this person will hit the dartboard? They are not particularly good. But in all probability, if he throws enough darts in the direction of the board, sooner or later he will eventually hit it.

What is the likelihood that this individual will hit a bull's-eye? If this person throws enough darts, if he stands there long enough, learns to adjust his aim over time, and keeps on throwing darts endlessly, he will, he must, eventually hit a bull's-eye.

This is one of the key lessons of life. No matter who you are or what situation you're starting from, if you try enough times, learn from every try, and persist over and over in aiming at a goal that's important to you, you must and will eventually hit a bull's-eye. It's not a matter of luck; it's simply a matter of probabilities.

Now imagine that you took this same person, cold sober, and gave him an advanced course in dart throwing by a professional dart player. You then put this person twelve or fifteen feet from the dartboard in a well-lit room, gave this person a large supply of beautifully crafted, highly accurate darts. This person thoughtfully and deliberately throws each dart, carefully adjusting his aim dart by dart. What would happen? Improving all of the controllable factors—knowledge, skill, lighting conditions, alertness, the clarity of the target, and the distance to the dartboard—would dramatically increase the probabilities that this individual would hit a bull's-eye far sooner than the first person.

By examining every part of the process of achieving the goals that are most important to you, and by taking each one of them into consideration and improving them as much as possible, you can dramatically increase the probabilities of achieving the success that you desire. If you want to be successful in any field, and you're absolutely clear, in writing, about what success means to you, you are much more likely to succeed. If you then study and develop the knowledge and skill necessary to excel in that field, you will further increase your probabilities of success. If you associate with the right people, manage yourself and your time extremely well, move quickly when opportunity presents itself, persevere in the face of obstacles, and take intelligent risks to accelerate your progress, you will put yourself on the side of the angels. You will improve your odds, and in one or two years you will achieve the success that other people may not achieve in ten or twenty years of less focused behavior. It's not a matter of luck. The law of averages says that, although you cannot predict which one of a series of events will be successful, by doing a certain thing a certain number of times, you will achieve your goal.

If you're absolutely clear about what success means,
you are much more likely to succeed.

For example, a woman arrives at an important event in a beautiful dress. It fits perfectly, the colors are perfectly matched to her skin tones and her hair, and it flatters her in every way; she looks terrific. A friend asks her, "Where did you get that lovely dress?"

She says, "I wanted to look my very best for this function, so I went out and shopped until I found the ideal dress."

Her friend says, "You were lucky to have found such an ideal dress for this event."

This woman thought clearly about the ideal dress for this party. She thought through her experience with clothes, colors, and fabrics. She gathered information by reading fashion magazines and looking at the ads. She phoned around to several stores to find out what they had in stock and in what sizes. She looked at a number of websites to see other options. She began a personal search and visited store after store, trying on various dresses and comparing them with her goal and her experiences. Eventually, well along in the process, she found a boutique in a distant shopping center that had exactly the right dress, in exactly the right color and size, with exactly the right cut for her.

Luck had nothing to do with this selection. This woman was perfectly clear about what she wanted, did her research thoroughly, used the telephone and Internet to save traveling time, and visited numerous places before she finally found exactly what she was looking for. The likelihood of her finding the ideal dress in any one store might have been low, but the law of averages said that if she looked in enough stores, with a clear idea of what she wanted, she would eventually find what she was looking for. If luck entered into the equation at all, it played only a small role.

The Law of Attraction

Perhaps the most important luck factor of all is the law of attraction. This law states that you are a living magnet and you inevitably attract into your life the people, circumstances, ideas, and resources that are in harmony with your dominant thoughts.

You inevitably attract into your life the people, circumstances, and resources that are in harmony with your dominant thoughts.

As you can see, the law of attraction is a direct extension of the law of cause and effect. In my experience, the law of attraction explains virtually every circumstance of your life. People who think and talk continually about what they want attract more and more of the things they want into their lives. People who condemn and complain, or who are envious, angry, and resentful, continually attract negative experiences.

Like the other laws, the law of attraction is neutral. These laws don't play favorites. They can work for you or against you, positively or negatively, depending on you. In fact, the most important life lesson you will ever learn is that your main job is to think and talk only about the things you want and discipline yourself to refuse to think and talk about the things that you don't want. This sounds simple, but it's often the most challenging and difficult thing you will ever attempt to do. We'll revisit this principle often throughout this book.

The Law of Belief

The law of belief is another luck factor that you can turn to your own advantage. Again, it can work for you or against you; it's up to you and how you apply it. The law of belief states that whatever you believe with conviction becomes your reality.

The great Harvard psychologist William James wrote that "belief creates the actual fact." The New Testament says, "According to your faith be it unto you" (Matthew 9:29). The Old Testament says, "For as he thinketh in his heart, so is he" (Proverbs 23:7). Throughout history, people have recognized that our beliefs play a major role in the way we see the world and the way we think and behave. If you absolutely believe that you're destined to be a great success in life, you will think and behave accordingly, and it will come true for you. If you absolutely believe that you're a lucky person and that good things are continually happening to you, your belief will become the actual fact of your life. Your beliefs do become your realities.

The Law of Mind

The law of mind, which is a corollary of the law of belief, says that thoughts objectify themselves. Your thoughts eventually materialize in the world around you. Jesus says, "By their fruits ye shall know them" (Matthew 7:20). You can tell what a person thinks about most of the time by looking at his or her life: a happy, healthy, prosperous person, with good friends and family, is invariably one who thinks about them in positive terms and believes that they are right and good for him or her.

Thoughts objectify themselves. Your thoughts
eventually materialize in the world around you.

Today there are more opportunities for people to achieve their goals, including health, happiness, and financial independence, than have existed in all of human history. Indeed one of the greatest luck factors, which few people realize or appreciate, is to have been born and to be alive in our world as it exists now. Never have there been more opportunities for more people to enjoy health and prosperity than today. Throughout all of history, men and women have dreamed of the Golden Age that we are just now entering. Of course, there will always be social, political, and economic problems, but these are inevitable, and they can be solved. The good news is that for you, the possibilities are unlimited.

The greatest limits on each person are self-limiting beliefs. Even though they are usually not based on fact at all, they cause you to sell yourself short. They act as brakes on your potential. Some of the most popular ones are, "I'm too old," "I'm too young," "I don't have enough education," "I have too much education," "I don't have enough experience," "I have too much experience." People think that they are not smart, creative, or talented enough to get the things they want.

Here's an important point: you cannot intensely desire something without simultaneously having the ability to attain it. The existence of the desire itself is usually proof that you have within you the ability to fulfill that desire. Your job is simply to find out how—to identify what you can do to increase the probabilities of achieving your goal, as you desire it, and on schedule.

The desire itself is usually proof that you have
within you the ability to fulfill that desire.

The Law of Expectations

Another luck factor is the law of expectations. It says that whatever you expect with confidence becomes your own self-fulfilling
prophecy. To paraphrase this law, you get not what you want in
life, but what you expect.

Fifty years of research have shown that the most powerful and
predictable personal motivational factor has been an attitude of
positive expectations. This is where you calmly and confidently
expect good things to happen to you. A great way to activate this
law in your life is to start off every morning by saying, *I believe
something wonderful is going to happen to me today.* Repeat this
affirmation several times until your entire mind is charged with
confident expectancy. At the end of the day, do a brief recap, and
look over the events of the past few hours. You'll be amazed to
notice the great number of wonderful things, large and small, that
did happen to you when your mind was supercharged with confident expectation.

Successful people are characterized by this attitude of self-
expectancy: they expect to succeed more often than they fail;
they expect to win more often than they lose; they expect to gain
something from every experience; they look for the good in every
situation. They see the glass as half full rather than half empty.
Even when things go wrong for them, they look into the setback
for the lessons they can learn and the advantages they can gain.

In his study of 500 of the richest men in America, Napoleon Hill, author of *Think and Grow Rich*, concluded that they all shared this attitude of positive expectancy. They made a habit of looking into every obstacle or setback for an equal or greater advantage or benefit, and they always found it. You must make a habit of doing the same.

If you start a career or business confidently expecting that people will buy from you, you will receive the funds that you require, and you will attract the best people to help you to realize your business dreams. Your attitude throughout the day goes before you like a shining light, affecting everybody that you come in contact with.

Your beliefs about yourself and your world affect your expectations; your expectations determine your attitude; your attitude determines your behavior; and your behavior toward other people determines how they relate to you. The more confident and positive you are, the more you believe yourself destined for great success, the more powerful the force of attraction will be; the more you will draw the people and circumstances you need to rapidly move ahead. People will continually call you lucky.

The Law of Subconscious Activity

The law of subconscious activity—another key luck factor—says that whatever thought or goal you hold in your conscious mind will be accepted by your subconscious mind as a command or instruction. Your subconscious mind, the seat of the law of attraction, will go to work to bring into your life the goals that you have set for yourself. Your subconscious mind will make your words and actions fit a pattern consistent with your self-concept: your dominant thoughts and ideas about yourself. Your subconscious mind will determine your body language and the way that you interact with other people. The commands you've given to your subconscious mind through your conscious mind will determine your tone of voice, your levels of energy and creativity, your enthusiasm, and your expectations. Your subconscious mind is extraordinarily powerful, and once it's directed to work for you at achieving specific goals and objectives, it will enable you to move forward at a speed that you cannot now imagine.

In your brain, there's a small fingerlike organ called the reticular cortex or reticular activating system. It is like a telephone switchboard: it takes in calls and passes them along to your conscious awareness as well as to your unconscious mind. It is activated by the commands that you pass from your conscious mind to your subconscious in the form of thoughts about who you are, what you want, and what is most important to you. It is activated by and makes your mind supersensitive to things you really want. For example, if you decide that you want a red sports car, you will begin to see red sports cars everywhere. If you decide to become financially successful, you will develop a selective perception for ideas, information, people, and opportunities that can help you financially. You will attract people who have ideas and advice for you, you will come across books and articles that answer key questions, and you'll begin behaving in ways that will set you up for financial success.

The Law of Affirmation

The law of affirmation is another luck factor that you can use continually. It simply says that whatever goals you repeat over and over in a positive, personal, present tense way will be accepted by your subconscious mind as commands. The results will then be drawn into your life by the law of attraction. For example, if you continue to repeat the words *I earn $150,000 per year, I earn $150,000 per year, I earn $150,000 per year* over and over, you will drive the idea deeper and deeper into your subconscious mind, which then accepts it, giving it a force of its own.

People who are described as lucky always tend to talk in positive terms about the things that they want and the circumstances that surround them. They recognize that, just as you become what you think about, you get what you talk about, so they make sure to talk about what they want, and not what they don't want.

The Law of Correspondences

The law of correspondence is perhaps my favorite of all the great timeless principles that explain success and failure. It is a key luck factor. It simply says that your outer world reflects your inner world; what is going on outside of you is a reflection or manifestation of what is going on inside of you.

Your outer world reflects your inner world. What is going on outside of you reflects what is going on inside of you.

When you stand in front of a mirror and see a reflection coming back at you, you know that it is determined by what you are presenting to the mirror. When you look at your life, you will find that it is primarily determined by who you are inside. Your relationships with other people, are largely determined by your character and personality. Your attitude and the way people react to you are largely determined by your beliefs and expectations about yourself and your world. Your wealth and financial attainment are determined by your inner level of aspiration and preparation. People are poor on the outside because they are poor on the inside. Your health on the outside is determined by the way you think about your health on the inside. People who think about food all the time tend to be overweight, unfit, and unhealthy. People who think about health and fitness all the time tend to be thin, trim, and energetic. It always begins with your thinking.

The Law of Mental Equivalents

The summary principle of all these laws is the law of mental equivalents. It says that your main job in life is to create within yourself the mental equivalent of what you wish to enjoy on the outside. You must build up the consciousness of success, health, happiness, prosperity, and personal achievement on the inside—thought by thought and feeling by feeling—that you wish to enjoy in the world around you.

Here's the great discovery: your past or future thoughts do not count. The only thing that makes a difference is the way you think at this very moment. You're not bound by the mistakes of the past or the limitations that you perceive in the future. Your potential is unlimited, because you are free to choose your thoughts at this moment, and what you think at this moment determines the future direction of your life. If you're driving down the road and you turn the wheel of your car in one direction, you will go in that direction from that moment on. The direction is not determined by how you drove yesterday or how you drive tomorrow; it is determined by the present moment.

You cannot control the entire world, you cannot control all the intricate and infinite details of modern life, you cannot control all the years of the past or all the years of the future, but you can control this present moment. That's all you need to do to achieve all the success that you can possibly imagine.

The Power of Suggestion

The power of suggestion is a luck factor as well. It says that your mind—that intricate combination of thoughts, feelings, words, pictures, images, ideas, insights, hopes, and fears—is continually changing. This change in your total mental makeup is either conscious, deliberate, and positive or random, haphazard, and negative.

The power of suggestion is the most powerful influence on everything you are and everything you become. As a result of the thousands of influences bombarding your mind every day, you are setting up a force field of attraction that is either bringing you the things you want or the things that you don't want. From now on, you must take conscious, systematic, purposeful control over the influences that you allow to reach your conscious mind. You must read healthy material, listen to positive audio programs, watch uplifting, educational video programs, and associate with positive people. You must guard your mental integrity as a sacred thing. Just as you would only eat healthy, nutritious foods if you wanted to be physically fit, you must only take in healthy, nutritious mental influences if you want to be mentally fit as well.

The Law of Responsibility

The final luck factor in this chapter is the law of responsibility. It states that you are 100 percent responsible for yourself, everything you are, and everything you become. You are where and what you are because you have decided to be there.

> You are 100 percent responsible for yourself,
> everything you are, and everything you become.

This law is the great liberator. It means that you are completely in charge of your life and everything that happens to you. Since you—and only you—can control your thinking, and your thinking controls your destiny, by taking charge of your thoughts you can control the rest of your life.

Luck is predictable; success is not an accident. Happiness or unhappiness are not accidents. They are predictable based on the laws that I've discussed in this chapter. Simply by deciding, you can become an extremely lucky person. You can think more of the thoughts that are consistent with what you want and do more of the things that increase your probabilities of success. At the same time, you can stop doing the things that are holding you back and accepting the ideas that are limiting your belief in your own potential.

If you buy a brand-new, beautifully engineered car and take it out on the road and it runs beautifully, do you ascribe it to luck? Of course not. Whether it is a beautiful automobile, a sophisticated piece of stereo machinery, or a handcrafted watch, you know that they have been built according to specific laws of mechanics, phys-ics, and electricity. The fact that they run beautifully is not luck.

It's the same with you. When you begin applying these luck factors to your life, you will start achieving extraordinary things. You will surge ahead of the people around you. You will enjoy greater success and achievement than you ever imagined, and it will be the result of design, not luck.

HOW TO BRING LUCK INTO YOUR LIFE

1. You can be successful at anything you want if you will simply do what successful people do.
2. The universe operates by the law of cause and effect. For everything that happens, there is a cause or series of causes that have brought it about.
3. Your choices in the past have brought you to where you are now.
4. You attract the circumstances of your life by your dominant thoughts.
5. Your mind is the most powerful force in the universe. By changing your thinking, you can change your life.
6. Whatever you believe with conviction becomes your reality.
7. Your main job is to create the mental equivalent of what you want to enjoy in life.

2

The Secret of Goals

Perhaps the most important of all luck factors is knowing exactly what you want in every area of your life. The number one reason for success is clear, specific, measurable goals, written down and backed by written plans and a burning desire to accomplish them. The primary reason for failure and underachievement is fuzziness, confusion, and the inability to decide exactly what you want, what it will look like, when you will want it, or how you will attain it. As the late motivational speaker Zig Ziglar used to say, the great majority of people are wandering generalities rather than meaningful specifics. You can't hit a target you can't see, and if you don't know where you're going, any road will get you there.

The number one reason for success
is clear, specific, written goals.

A person with no clear goals is like a ship without a rudder, carried whichever way the tides and wind are blowing. But a person with clear, specific goals is like a ship with a rudder, sailing straight and true to its destination. It's amazing how fast you will change your luck by becoming intensely goal-oriented. As a friend of mine once said, "Success is goals, and all else is commentary." It may not be as simple as that, but that is a wonderful place to start.

One recent best seller proclaims that "coincidences actually do happen." This is supposed to be a great revelation, and many people have become excited at this thought, but in most cases, coincidences don't happen. There are instead a variety of differing probabilities for the occurrences of particular events. Based on the law of averages, if you do enough different things over the course of the years, like billiard balls rolling around, one or two of them are going to bang into each other, but it is based on law, not luck or coincidence.

The Law of Serendipity

There are two extraordinarily important principles for you to learn. They are essential luck factors and have been throughout history. They are practiced by the most successful men and women alive today. Understanding them can open your eyes to potentials and possibilities that you may have never been aware of in the past.

The first of these luck factors is the principle of *serendipity*. Serendipity has best been described as the capacity for making happy discoveries along the road of life.

The word *serendipity* comes from the fairy tale of the three princes of Serendip or Serendib (today's Sri Lanka). These three princes would travel around, coming on experience after experience of misfortune and seeming disaster in the lives of others. But as a result of their visit and their changing the mind of the unfortunate person, the disaster was turned into a success.

For example, the three princes came to a farmhouse where a sad accident had taken place. The farmer's only son had been thrown from the farmer's only horse and broken his leg. The horse had run off and could not be found. As you can imagine, the farmer was quite distressed, but the three princes told him not to worry; something good would come out of it.

This country happened to be involved in a war with a neighboring country. The next morning, a squad of soldiers arrived to conscript all young, able-bodied men into the army. Because the farmer's only son had a broken leg, he was spared from conscription. Later that day, representatives of the government came by to seize all horses that could be used by the army, but since his only horse had run off, again the farmer was spared.

These apparently unfortunate events turned out to be the farmer's salvation. After the government representatives had left, the horse came home on his own accord, the son's leg soon mended, and the farmer was happy. But the army lost a great battle, and most of the horses and men were killed.

In another case, the three princes came across a wealthy landowner whose entire estate had been washed away by a flood. Everything he had accumulated in his lifetime was destroyed. As you can imagine, he was distraught and depressed, but the three princes convinced him that something good would turn up.

Not long after, as they walked across the battered, flooded land, where all the topsoil had been washed away by the flood, they found a precious stone, and then another, and another. The flood, washing away layers of old topsoil, revealed countless precious stones that made the landowner wealthier than he had ever imagined.

The key to the principle of serendipity is contained in the law of positive expectations: the more confidently you expect something good to come out of every situation, the more likely it is to occur.

The more confidently you expect something good to come out of every situation, the more likely it is to occur.

The serendipity principle only operates when you are absolutely confident that all will work out for the better. Then all kinds of happy occurrences take place. Many of them may seem like setbacks or failures, but they turn out to be exactly what had to happen for you to achieve your goal.

Here is an important philosophical principle: your situation today is exactly what you need at this moment for your own personal growth and development. Every part of your life is exactly as it should be. Everything you are dealing with contains possibilities that you can turn to your own advantage.

You may be working for a difficult boss in an industry where the competition is fierce, the margins are low, and the potential future is limited. If you are not careful, you will allow yourself to become negative about your current situation, but if you realize that according to the principle of serendipity, it's exactly what you need at this moment, you can look for the advantage it might contain.

You can ask yourself, "If I were not doing this job, knowing what I now know about this job and its future, would I get into this field in the first place?" If your answer is no, then your next question could be, "If I could do anything I really wanted, what would it be?" Whatever it is, you can use your current experience as a springboard to higher and better experiences rather than just sitting there wishing and hoping that things will improve.

One great luck factor is the law of futurity, which says that it doesn't matter where you're coming from; all that matters is where you're going. The past is dead. It serves only to give you guidance and wisdom so you can make better decisions in the future. You can't allow yourself to cry over spilled milk. Look upon the past as a sunk cost, as an irretrievable investment in your future. Then turn your eyes toward the future horizon of your own possibilities and begin moving in that direction.

The past is dead. It serves only to give you guidance and wisdom for making better decisions in the future.

The Principle of Synchronicity

The second principle is perhaps the most important luck factor of all, and it is intertwined with many of the other principles in this book. It is called *synchronicity*. It goes above and beyond the law of cause and effect, which says that every effect in your life has certain specific causes that you can trace back and identify.

The principle of synchronicity, on the other hand, says that things will happen that have no direct cause and effect relationship. Events are often linked not by causality but by meaning. For example, you get up one morning, and you begin talking with your spouse about taking a vacation to Hawaii, but you know you can't afford it and you can't get the time off anyway. Nonetheless, the idea of going to Hawaii is very exciting to you. Because it is, you emotionalize the idea of a Hawaiian vacation. Any thought you emotionalize is passed from your conscious mind to your subconscious mind, the seat of the law of attraction. As a result, you send out positive vibrations, which attract people and circumstances that will make that thought a reality.

You go to work that day, and in passing you mention that you would like to take a trip to Hawaii with your spouse sometime. Your boss calls you in a couple of hours later and tells you that since you have been doing such a great job and the company is in a slow season, it will be no problem at all if you want to take a week or two off for vacation. At lunchtime the same day, a friend tells you about a new travel agency that puts together Hawaiian vacation packages, including hotel, airfare, and ground transportation at great prices. In fact, your friend has a brochure describing exactly the island that you wanted to visit and the hotel that would be ideal for you, and the price is less than $2,000 for both of you for an entire week in Hawaii. That night, you get home and there is an income-tax refund in the mail for an unexpected overpayment that amounts to—you guessed it—$2,000.

Notice what has happened. You had a very clear, emotionally charged thought of taking a trip to Hawaii with your spouse. That day, three events occurred, none of them having any causal connection with the others but all of which came together to enable you to achieve your goal in less than one day. This sort of thing happens all the time once you get into "the zone." When you emotionalize your mind, clarify your thoughts, intensify your desires, and approach your life with confident, positive expectation, all sorts of serendipitous and synchronous events begin to happen to you.

The only relationship these events have to one another is the meaning that you give them by your thoughts about the things you really want. But if your thoughts are fuzzy, confused, and contradictory, these principles can't work for you. This is the primary reason why most people are unhappy and unsuccessful. They have enormous powers, but they fail to use them because they don't understand how they work.

Over and over, it's been found that corporations with very clear, written strategic plans are far more successful than those that are operating from the seat of their pants. Now it takes a good deal of time—sometimes many hours and even many days—to write out a strategic plan, but it is a blueprint for the future of the company. The purpose of all strategic planning is to increase the return on equity, the return on investment, or on capital invested in the business.

By the same token, you will be far more effective when you have a personal strategic plan, but instead of designing a plan to increase your return on equity, your job is to increase your return on energy. Just as a company has financial capital to invest in the marketplace, you have human capital to invest in your life. Your human capital is mental, emotional, and physical, and your job is to get the highest possible return on your investment of this personal capital in the months and years that you invest in your adult life.

> You will be far more effective when
> you have a personal strategic plan.

In every industry, there are people who are doing very much the same job but who are earning far more or far less than others.

It's common for me to meet two people selling the same product, out of the same office, under the same competitive conditions, to the same people, at the same prices, but one of them is earning three, four, five, even ten times as much as the other, even though there is virtually no difference in age, education, experience, intelligence, or anything else. Why?

You already know part of the answer: it's because the more successful person has done many little things to increase the likelihood of success. The less successful person has failed to do these things. Just as you reap what you sow, you fail to reap what you don't sow. If you don't put it in, you don't get it out. If you do not trigger the action, you don't get the reaction.

Almost invariably, the highest-paid people in America have personal strategic plans. These people are intensely goal-oriented. They know exactly what they want. They have written plans, blueprints, and outlines, and ideas to achieve these plans. The more clear you are about what you want, and the more excited you are about achieving it, the more you will activate the laws of belief, expectation, attraction, correspondence, and mental equivalence, and the more you will enjoy serendipity and synchronicity; the more your life will become a continuous series of happy circumstances that move you toward your goal and move your goal toward you.

The Law of Control

The law of control is a key luck factor. It says that you feel positive about yourself to the degree to which you feel you are in control of your own life; you feel negative about yourself to the degree to which you feel you are controlled by external forces or other people. There is a direct relationship between high performance and happiness on the one hand and a sense of control in your life on the other. The more you feel you are in charge of what is happening to you, the more you feel you are the architect of your destiny and the master of your fate. The more you feel you're in charge of your life, the happier, more positive, more energetic, and more focused you will be.

> There is a direct relationship between happiness and the feeling of being in control of your life.

If you feel that you are controlled by your boss, your bills, your health, your relationships, your upbringing, your race, or any other factor, you will feel out of control; you will feel anxious, negative, and angry; you will lash out and blame other people for your problems; you will resent successful people; and you will envy anyone who is doing better than you are. You will set yourself up for failure because you will attract into your life the negative things that you think about all day long.

Clear, written goals give you a sense of control over the direction of change in your life. They give you the feeling that you are in the driver's seat, that you have your hands on the wheel, that your life is going where you want it to go. The more you feel in control of your life, the more positive and optimistic you become. The more positive you become and the clearer you are about what you want and where you're going, the more you activate the mental laws on your behalf, and the more luck you will seem to experience.

The Law of Purpose

The law of purpose says that the secret of success is constancy of purpose; all really successful people are characterized by intensity of purpose. Given two people with roughly the same abilities and opportunities, the one who wants it more intensely is the one who will almost always be the more successful. Your job is to decide what you really want in every area of your life. Then focus intensely on it like a laser beam and stay on it, no matter how long it takes until you achieve it.

The law of accident is the opposite of the law of control. It says that failing to plan means planning to fail. People who live by the law of accident believe that life is a series of random, haphazard chances, like the throwing of dice or the turning of a roulette wheel. They believe that it's not what you know but who you know, that you can't fight city hall. People who live by the law of accident buy lottery tickets, go to casinos, invest in get-rich-quick schemes, penny stocks, and things they don't know anything about. They're always hoping for a lucky break and never getting one. People who live by the law of accident are usually the most envious of those who are successfully living by the law of control.

Although most people live by the law of accident, you can free yourself from it in an instant. In putting together your own personal strategic plan, you start from the inside and work outward. You start from the inner core of your being, your innermost values and convictions, and then you organize every aspect of your external life so that what you are doing on the outside is congruent with your fundamental unifying principles.

The Law of Clarity

The law of clarity says that the clearer you are about what you want, the more rapidly you will attain it. Your ability to focus single-mindedly on one thing at a time and stay with it until it is complete is a key luck factor. It increases your likelihood of having fortuitous events occur that help you to achieve your goals.

I've found that people with goals are far more interesting and optimistic than people without them. Everyone wants to be happy, but almost every unhappy person will confess that they don't have any goals. People without goals tend to be negative and unhappy and complain continually about a variety of things. When somebody complains about some part of their life, you can simply ask, "What are your goals?" They may say they are unhappy about their jobs, their marriages, their health, their relationships, or something else, but when you ask them what they would really like to be, have, or do, they're flabbergasted; they have no idea. Sometimes they are offended that you would even ask them such a question.

Values and Mission

What are your values? What do you believe in? What do you stand for? Equally importantly, what would you *not* stand for? Do you believe in the importance of honesty, sincerity, generosity, compassion, caring, love, forgiveness, and truth? Do you believe in the importance of integrity, personal excellence, creativity, freedom, and self-expression? Do you believe in friendship, self-discipline, work, self-development, and success?

Your ability to ask and answer these questions for yourself is the key to your success. It is indispensable to finding exactly what you really want and what you are willing to work for. You don't need more than three to five basic values; this much is sufficient. Once you've selected your key values, you need to organize them by priority. Which comes first? Which comes second? Which comes third?

How can you tell what your values are today? It's easy. You always express your values in your actions. You tell yourself and others what you truly believe by what you do under pressure. Whenever you're forced to choose to go one way or the other, you always go in the direction that is consistent with your dominant value at the time. If a person says that, "My family is my most important value," this means that, when forced to choose, he will always pick his family. If a person believes that health is his key value, he will always act to maintain the health and well-being of both himself and the people he most cares about. It's not what you say or wish or hope or intend or plan to do or be someday; it's only what you say and do each moment that truly indicates your fundamental values and convictions.

Once you have determined your values, you move to your vision and your mission statement. Your vision is a written description of how you want to be perceived by others in the future. Some people suggest that you write out your own obituary: what you would want to be read by a trusted friend at your graveside.

A vision statement is an ideal description of the very best person you could possibly imagine becoming over the course of your lifetime. The wonderful thing about a vision statement is that once you write it and then read it and review it on a regular basis, it activates the mental laws, and you start to become the kind of person that you have imagined. By writing out a vision statement, you take responsibility for shaping your character and destiny. Remember, you become what you think about most of the time. If you think about yourself as an excellent human being, over time, you will become very much like the person you have decided to become.

The Law of Desire

The law of desire says that the only limitation on your abilities is how badly you really want something. Your desire determines your destiny. The fire of desire determines your constancy and intensity of purpose. A person with a burning desire to achieve a goal of any kind will find himself or herself automatically driven toward it.

> The only limitation on your abilities is
> how badly you really want something.

Desire is the fuel of ambition. Desire is the power in your personality. The primary reason people don't accomplish much is that they're not passionate enough about what they want to be, have, or do; they don't desire it enough.

The only way you can have an intense, burning desire for a specific goal, personal or otherwise, is for that goal to be an expression of your true values. It must be consistent with your vision of the person you really want to become in your life.

Your mission, on the other hand, is a little different from your vision. Your mission is a specific statement of what you want to accomplish with your life sometime in the future. Your mission statement describes how you want to make a difference with your life.

The only way to make a difference with your life is by figuring out how you're going to make a difference in the lives of other people. When Albert Einstein was asked the purpose of human life, he replied, "Why, it must be to serve others; what other purpose could there be?"

A mission is not only attainable but measurable. It's not a vague set of warm generalities that make people feel good but cannot be applied or measured in practice. For example, at one time the mission statement of AT&T was to bring a telephone within the reach of every person in America. It took the company almost eighty years to achieve that goal.

Your mission could be something like this: *I am an outstanding, professional salesperson, among the top 10 percent in my industry. I give the very finest quantity and quality of service, reliability, and honesty to every customer, and as a result I earn more than $150,000 per year.*

This mission statement tells the level you want to attain in your field, the kind of work that you're going to do to attain that level, and how you will measure your achievement of that goal.

Your Dream List

Here is a wonderful exercise for you. Take a piece of paper and write out your dream list. Let your mind float freely. Imagine that you have no limitations. Imagine that you have all the time, all the money, all the resources, all the intelligence, all the education, all the experience, and all the contacts in the world. Imagine that you could do, be, or have anything in your life.

Now write down everything you would want in your life if you had no limitations whatsoever. Be sure to decide what is *right for you* before you decide what is *possible*. Don't fall into the loser's trap of shooting yourself in the foot by thinking of all the reasons why it's not possible before you even begin writing. Put the word *possible* aside for now and just allow yourself to dream.

Leaders in every field have vision. They allow themselves to dream and see a vision of what could be rather than allowing themselves to get stuck with what exists at the present moment.

Once you have finished your dream list, take another sheet of paper and write today's date at the top. Then write down at least ten goals that you want to accomplish in the next twelve months.

This is one of the most powerful exercises I've ever learned. It changed my life when I began using it many years ago. I wasn't really sure that it would work when I began toying with it, but all it cost me was a few minutes and a piece of paper, and my life has been different ever since.

When you make out a list of ten goals that you want to accomplish in the next twelve months, you automatically move yourself into the top 3 percent of Americans. Since only 3 percent of adult Americans will ever write down their goals, you have joined the elite by the very act of writing down ten things you want. Even if all you did was to put that sheet of paper away somewhere for a year, your whole life would be different. At the end of twelve months, when you opened up that sheet of paper, you'd be astonished to find that fully 80 percent of the ten goals had been achieved in the most remarkable ways. In fact, you would probably see examples of synchronicity and serendipity behind the attainment of each of those goals. You would see a remarkable string of interconnected coincidences that no one could predict or plan for. You will have accomplished 80 percent of your ten goals in ways that you cannot now even imagine.

Your Major Definite Purpose

The next exercise is to take that list of ten goals and go through it, asking yourself, "Which one goal, if I accomplish it, would have the greatest positive impact on my life?" Circle that goal and write it down on the top of another sheet of paper. This becomes your major definite purpose for the time being.

Remember, the law of purpose says that the secret of success is constancy of purpose. By writing down ten goals, selecting your most important one, and deciding upon that as your major definite purpose, you have now moved into the top 1 percent of Americans living today.

Below your goal, on that sheet of paper, write out every single action that you can possibly think of that you could do now or in the future to achieve that goal. This is a very important exercise. The more things that you write down that could help you achieve your goal, the more you will begin to believe that it is possible for you.

When you write down the goal for the first time, you may have a lot of hope, but you will probably be skeptical of your ability to achieve it. When you write down all the different things that you could do to achieve your goal, starting today, you begin to see your goal in a whole new light. As you write down idea after idea, you drive the goal deeper and deeper into your subconscious mind; you begin to believe that it's possible for you.

As you do different things on your list, you begin to expect that you will move toward your goal. Activating the law of attraction, you attract people and circumstances into your life that help you to achieve your goal. You see examples of synchronicity in the events and circumstances that surround you. You feel more in control of your life. You activate your reticular cortex, and you develop an intense sensitivity and awareness to people and possibilities around you that can help you to achieve that objective. You feel more alert and aware and alive, you have more energy and focus, you're clearer and more positive, and all it takes is a piece of paper and a few minutes of your time.

There are many differences between winners and losers. The loser always hears a piece of advice and asks, "What if it doesn't work?" But that's the wrong question. The right question for you to ask is, "What if it does?"

If it doesn't work, all it cost you is a piece of paper. (But you would have to be a determinedly negative person to stop this exercise from working in spite of yourself.) However, the fact is that it does work, and faster than you could imagine.

The Law of Accelerating Acceleration

A financial advisor attended my seminar in Phoenix on a Saturday morning. He flew back to Houston that afternoon. The following Thursday, he phoned my office and spoke to my secretary. Then he wrote me a letter in some detail which told what he had done after he had left the seminar. This is what happened to him.

He said that he had heard about goals many times before, but he had never thought about writing them down. He decided that, as a result of my recommendation, he would write down ten goals for the next twelve months, which he did. He said that by Sunday night at seven o'clock, in less than forty-eight hours, he had already accomplished five of the ten one-year goals he had set for himself (and these were both financial goals and family goals). He quickly wrote out five more goals, so that he had a new, complete list of ten goals.

By Thursday evening at five o'clock, when he called my office four days later, he had already accomplished five more of the items on his new list. In his letter he wrote, "I can quite honestly say that I accomplished more in six days with clear, written goals than I had honestly expected to accomplish in an entire year. I was simply amazed."

The process of goal setting boils down to the specific actions that you are going to take now, today, and every day to achieve your goals. Once you have them written out, you can use a series of powerful mental techniques to accelerate your progress toward your goals and to move them more rapidly toward yourself.

The law of accelerating acceleration applies to almost every big goal that you set for yourself. It says that whatever you are moving toward is moving toward you as well; like attracts like. In a way this is a corollary of the law of attraction, but with one important difference: as you begin to move toward your goal, you will be frustrated at how slow it seems to be. The bigger your goal, the further away it will seem. You will have to work at it a long time before you see any progress at all, but this is all part of the process of goal attainment.

Whatever you are moving toward is moving
toward you as well. Like attracts like.

The 20/80 rule applies to the law of accelerating acceleration. It says that in the first 80 percent of the time that you are working toward your goal, you will only cover about 20 percent of the distance. However, if you keep on keeping on, you will accomplish the final 80 percent of your goal in the last 20 percent of the time that you spend working toward it.

Many people work for weeks, months, and even years toward a big goal and see very little progress. They lose heart and give up. But they didn't realize that they had laid all of the groundwork necessary; they were almost at the takeoff point where they would begin to move at an extraordinary speed toward their goal and their goal would begin to move at an extraordinary speed toward them.

Take your major goals and write them down as positive affirmations in a first-person, present-tense form on a series of 3 x 5 index cards. This is an incredibly powerful exercise. It's like jamming your foot onto the accelerator of your life. For example, you could write, "I weigh 150 pounds" on one card; "I earned $150,000 per year" on another card; and "I speak Spanish fluently" on another.

Whatever your goals are, write them down in large letters on 3 x 5 index cards and carry the cards around with you. Read and reread these goal cards each morning and evening when you get up and before you go to bed. As you read them, visualize each goal as if it were already attained. Get a clear mental picture of your goal as a reality. See it as vividly and clearly as you can. And here's the kicker: combine the mental picture of your goal with the feeling you would expect to enjoy if your goal were already a reality.

As you create a mental picture of the beautiful car you want to drive, create the feeling of pride, happiness, satisfaction, and pleasure that you would enjoy as you drove away in that car. Many top salespeople have told me that they used this exercise by visualizing themselves as the top salesperson for the company and winning the award at the national sales convention. They visualized and imagined themselves walking up onto the stage and receiving the award from the company president. They heard the audience. They created the feeling of pride and satisfaction that they would enjoy when they attained that award. Over and over, these people became the top performers in their organizations.

The Law of Concentration

Another tremendous luck factor is contained in the principle of attention, or the law of concentration. This law states that whatever you dwell upon grows and increases in your world. The more you think about, talk about, visualize, and emotionalize a desired goal, the more your mental capacity works to draw that goal toward you and to draw you toward that goal. The clearer you are about your goals, the more you write them and rewrite them, the more you plan them and work on them, the more you activate all of your mental powers to create a force field of energy that causes wonderful things to happen to you. You attract amazing opportunities and possibilities that other people think of as luck.

Whatever you dwell upon grows and increases in your world.

The fact that you are reading this book means that you are already in the top 10 percent, perhaps the top 5 percent, of people living today. You are among what has been called "the talented tenth." You're a member of the elite. You are the kind of person who is constantly learning and growing. You are in a special class. You are in the winner's circle. It doesn't matter where you are in life or how much you're earning today; all that matters is where you're going.

The commitment that you are making to your life and your future is the surest indicator of where you're going to be in a few years. If you keep on keeping on in the same direction that you're going in now, you will accomplish extraordinary things, and nothing can stop you. You will become known as one of the luckiest people in your world.

KEYS TO GOAL SETTING

1. The most important of all luck factors is knowing exactly what you want.

2. Your expectations shape every event and situation in your life.

3. It doesn't matter where you're coming from. All that matters is where you're going.

4. The principle of synchronicity says that things will happen that have no direct cause and effect relationship. Events are often linked not by causality but by meaning.

5. A personal strategic plan is key to your success.

6. Clear, written goals give you a sense of control over the direction of your life.

7. Write down your major goals as positive affirmations in a first-person, present-tense form on a series of 3 x 5 index cards.

3

Knowledge: The Key to Power and Success

There is a race on today. You are in it, and the only question is whether or not you're going to win or lose. This is up to you. Your advantage is that the great majority of other people don't realize that they're in a race to the finish. And they either don't know how to compete, or they're not aware of how important it is to win. It took 6,000 years of recorded history for man to move from the agricultural age into the industrial age, which began around 1760. By 1950, the majority of employees in the advanced countries were industrial workers. But by 1960, the industrial age was over, and we had entered into the service age. There were more people delivering services than there were in manufacturing.

By the late seventies, we had entered into the information age. In the twenty-first century, we are in the communications age. There are more people employed now in communicating information, ideas, entertainment, news, or education than in any other single industry. We've gone from muscle power to mind power, from brute power to brainpower. For the rest of your life, the knowledge content of everything you do is going to determine the quality and quantity of your work and your life.

The Proliferation of Information

According to Moore's law, information processing capacity doubles every eighteen months and drops by half in cost during the same time. What this means is incredible. If the cost of a new Lexus automobile had kept pace with the cost of computing capacity, a new Lexus today would cost $2, get 700 miles from a gallon of gas, and travel at 500 miles per hour. In fact, a new Lexus today has more computer systems in it than the Apollo 13, which was the most advanced moon rocket of its time. In a new automobile today, more money is spent on electronics than on steel.

We've moved into the information age, with knowledge as the primary source of value, so fast that most of the major institutions of society have not yet caught up or caught on. Financial institutions today, banks especially, are baffled by the fact that a $100 million factory can be rendered obsolete with a change in technology in as little as eighteen months.

Today knowledge is the primary source of value.

Brainpower can be used in an infinite number of ways to create wealth, with virtually no investment in fixed assets. When a financial institution today asks for collateral, it has no way of measuring the fact that the company's most valuable assets are between the ears of the people who work there. The entire organization could burn to the ground tomorrow, and the brainpower could walk across the street and start over again in a few hours.

The Winning Edge

You may have heard of the concept of the winning edge. It says that small differences in knowledge and ability can lead to enormous differences in results. One small piece of information that you have but your competitors lack can be all that it takes for you to gain the winning edge.

One example is a horse race. If a horse comes in first by a nose, it wins ten times as much as the horse that comes in second. Does this mean that the winning horse is ten times faster? Twice as fast? Ten percent faster? No. The horse that wins is only a nose faster. But a nose translates into ten times the prize money.

In a competitive market, when a company gets a sale, it is often only a tiny bit better than the company that loses, but the winning company gets 100 percent of the sale and 100 percent of the profit. Is this company 100 percent better than the one that loses the deal? No. It has merely developed a winning edge, but that makes all the difference.

Another key luck factor is the law of integrative complexity. This law says that in every group, the individual who can integrate the greatest amount of information will rise and dominate all the others in that group. To put it another way, the more knowledge and experience a person has, the more patterns he or she can recognize and act upon in any given set of circumstances. The person with the greatest ability for pattern recognition will always rise to the top of any organization, because his or her contribution will be of greater value and have greater impact than that of anyone else.

The top salespeople tend to remain the top salespeople. Why? Because they've worked many weeks, months, and years to become more and more skilled at selling ever more competitive products to ever more sophisticated and demanding customers. As a result, like runners gaining an edge and increasing it as the race goes on, the top salespeople pull ahead—often way ahead of their competitors. It's because they have been exposed to more and more patterns in more and more complex and varied sales. This enables them to sell more and more. As you've heard, nothing succeeds like success.

As knowledge in your field more rapidly expands, your store of knowledge more rapidly becomes obsolete. If you were to take a trip around the world in a catamaran and were gone for a year or two, when you got back you would find that perhaps 50 percent of all the knowledge that you had accumulated that justified your salary and position was no longer of any use anymore.

Admittedly, some fields have rates of knowledge obsolescence that are far faster than others. Knowledge in a slowly changing field may take ten or twenty years or even longer to become obsolete. However, a stockbroker's knowledge of prices, market positions, interest rates, economic dynamics, and other factors may become completely obsolete in a few weeks or even a few days. One political event can make the accumulated knowledge of how an election is going to turn out obsolete overnight.

The future belongs to the competent. It does not belong to the well-meaning, the sincere, or the merely ambitious; it belongs to those who are very good at what they do. There's an old saying that the rich get richer and the poor get poorer. Today, however, it is not a contest between those who have more and those who have less; it is between those who know more and those who know less.

The future does not belong to the well-meaning,
the sincere, or the merely ambitious. It belongs
to those who are very good at what they do.

The most significant differences in income in America are between those who have continually increased their levels of knowledge and skill and those who have not. To earn more, you must learn more. You are maxed out today at your current level of knowledge and skill. If you want to increase your income and your earning ability, you have to learn more new, valuable information and ideas that you can apply in the marketplace to create value. It's often been said that knowledge is power. The fact is that only applied knowledge is power. Only knowledge that can be utilized to bring about a benefit that someone will pay for is power in today's marketplace. And how do you evaluate a piece of knowledge? Simple. Valuable knowledge increases your ability to get results for other people.

There are enormous quantities of knowledge taught in universities that are true but useless in the real world. College graduates are frequently shocked to find that they have spent three or four years learning about subjects that few others care about. This is why fully 80 percent of college graduates find themselves working outside their fields of study within two years of leaving school.

As I mentioned earlier, I started off with very few advantages in life, but I had one thing: I liked to read. Over time, I got hooked on reading and learning. Over the years, I found that virtually every successful person in America who has started with nothing and worked his way up, has done it through a commitment to personal development and personal growth.

The law of self-development says that you can learn anything you need to learn to achieve any goal you set for yourself. This is one of the great laws of success. It means that there are no limitations on what you can accomplish. If you can be clear about your goal, you can identify the knowledge you need to achieve it. By acquiring that knowledge, the achievement of your goal becomes inevitable.

Just imagine: you can start off with nothing but an intense desire to be successful and through self-study and self-development, you can learn anything you need to learn to achieve any goal you set for yourself. Ninety percent of all fortunes today are still made in regular businesses, selling established products and services in established markets to established customers. All you really need to start a fortune is an idea that is 10 percent new—a new piece of knowledge, a new idea, a new insight—and the willingness and ability to apply it in the marketplace, and you can become a big success in our economic system. Abraham Lincoln once wrote, "I will study and prepare myself, and someday my chance will come."

Luck occurs when preparation meets opportunity. Many people are sitting around waiting for a lucky break, but people do not just have lucky breaks. They create their lucky breaks by preparing so thoroughly for their opportunity that when it comes along, they're ready to grasp and run with it. Inspirational speaker Earl Nightingale once said, "If your opportunity comes and you are not prepared for it, you will only look foolish." But by the law of attraction, when you do put in the preparation, you will attract into your life an opportunity to use your knowledge and skills at the level you're ready for.

Luck occurs when preparation meets opportunity.

The Law of Talents

The law of talents says, to quote motivational speaker Jim Rohn, that if you develop your talents, they will make a way for you. You will never develop a useful talent or ability without, sooner or later, having an opportunity to apply it to some good purpose. You will draw into your life the people, circumstances, opportunities, and resources necessary for you to apply the talent that you worked so hard to develop.

The law of variety, as it applies to ideas, says that your success will be determined by the quality and quantity of ideas that you can generate to improve your circumstances. Ideas are the keys to the future; they are the primary source of value; they are the cream of knowledge rising to the top. But ideas in and of themselves have no value. It's only your ability to take an idea and execute it in such a way that you can bring about valuable improvement that adds worth to it.

I'm always amazed when people try to sell me their new idea. I ask them what it is. They tell me that they can't tell me until I've paid for it. I explain to them that their ideas are of no value by themselves, because ninety-nine out of 100 ideas don't work. And the one idea that does work only has value when it is combined with other ideas and resources to achieve some worthy end.

Your Knowledge Advantage

With regard to knowledge, you have a distinct advantage. The great majority of people are drifting along hopelessly unaware that their knowledge is limited and is becoming obsolete more and more every day. They spend most of their time socializing at work and at home, watching television, and living as easy a life as possible. However, the small, intelligent minority like you, who realize that we're in a race for useful knowledge, have the winning edge. You are already ahead of the pack, because you realize what you need to do to move to the top of your field. If you want to know how high they're going to build an office building, you can tell by looking at how deep they dig the foundation. The depth of the foundation determines how high the structure can be erected. But once the building is complete, the owners cannot go back and add on another twenty or thirty floors by digging the foundation deeper. It's too late for that.

The Intellectual Foundation

The same principle holds true with you. You can tell how high you will rise in life by how deeply you dig your intellectual foundation. And you can continually increase the height of your personal life structure by continually increasing the depth of your knowledge and understanding; there are virtually no limits. You attract good luck by the quality of your thinking, and the quality of your thinking is determined by your commitment to continuous learning. The more you soak your mind in new knowledge, new insights, new ideas, and new information, the more your mind will be stimulated and magnetized to attract all kinds of opportunities and possibilities to help you achieve your goals and live a great life.

You can tell how high you will rise in life by how
deeply you dig your intellectual foundation.

The key to expanding your knowledge is reading. Perhaps not all readers are leaders, but all leaders are readers. How much do you read? The highest-paid Americans read an average of two to three hours per day. The lowest-paid Americans don't read at all. According to the American Booksellers Association, 80 percent of American families did not buy or read a single book in the last year, 70 percent of American adults have not been into a bookstore in the last five years, and 58 percent of adults never read another book after they leave high school, including 42 percent of university graduates. According to *USA Today*, 43.6 percent of American adults read below the seventh-grade level. For all intents and purposes, this means that they are functionally illiterate. Fully 50 percent of high school graduates can neither read their graduation diplomas nor fill out an application form for a job at McDonald's. Many large companies that advertise, continually looking for qualified people, are forced to reject 95 percent of all applicants because they lack basic reading skills.

In America in 2022, $25.8 billion was spent on the movie industry. If you look around, you will see movie stars and movie industry news in every newspaper and magazine. They are the constant subject of news and entertainment. It is as though we are surrounded by and immersed in a movie culture. But you probably don't know that in 2022, Americans spent more than $29 billion on books. They purchase around 900 million books from all sources. In fact, this knowledge age has been dubbed the age of the book.

If you go into the home of a wealthy person, what's the first thing you see? A library. The wealthier the people and the larger the home, the more likely they are to have a large, fully stocked library. If you go into the home of poor people, what's the first thing you see? That's right—the biggest darn television they can afford.

Did the people become wealthy and then buy the books? Or did they buy the books, read them, and then become wealthy? I think the answer is clear. I had a friend who graduated from high school without learning to read. He was upset to find that the only jobs he could get were minimum wage, laboring jobs: digging ditches, planting trees, and sweeping floors. He came from a good home and a good neighborhood, but all he could get was dead-end jobs. All his friends who got out of high school without learning to read were in the same situation.

After a year and a half of this frustrating work, he came to me and asked for my advice. I told him that he needed to upgrade his education. He told me that he didn't really like to read; reading big paragraphs made him tired. I told him that he had better go to a community college and take a course on reading. He was reluctant to do it, but he was even more reluctant to continue working as a laborer. So he went to a community college at night for two years. He learned how to read proficiently. As a result, he applied to a technical school and took a degree in biomedical electronics. It took him two more years to graduate. But he was then immediately hired by a large hospital supply company to sell medical instrumentation to hospitals and clinics. Within five years, he was earning a great salary; he had a home, a car and, a great life. He later told me that the advice to learn to read and upgrade his education was the turning point in his career.

Here are some keys for upgrading your knowledge through reading. They've been successful for me and for thousands of other highly paid leaders in their industries. The best books to read are those written by men and women who are actively working in their fields. They are books written by experts, by practitioners of their crafts. Stay away from books written by university professors and management consultants. These people usually do not have the in-depth understanding that comes from working all day long, year after year, in a particular field.

You can buy a book full of ideas that someone else has taken twenty years to learn and has then written about. For the price of a book, you can get the knowledge that has cost the author years of time and thousands of dollars to accumulate.

For the price of a book, you can get the knowledge that has cost the author years of time and thousands of dollars to accumulate.

One Good Idea Can Change Your Life

All you need is one good idea to change the course of your life. Every problem that you could ever have has already been solved by someone somewhere. That solution is written in a book or magazine, and it's available to you if you can find it. But if there's an idea out there that can save you thousands of dollars and years of hard work and you don't have that idea, it's as if it didn't exist at all. This is why successful people are continually bombarding their minds with new information and new ideas. You may be exposed to a hundred ideas before you're hit by the one that you need at that moment. It requires a large quantity of ideas to find one or two quality insights.

Build your own library; buy your own books; don't check them out and then take them back. Underline the key points with a colored pen or highlighter. Make the books your own property. When I first started buying and marking up my own books, I found that it might take me a few hours to read a book the first time, but then I could read all of the key points through in less than an hour. Now I quickly read a book and dictate the most valuable ideas to be typed up and reviewed later.

The OPIR Method

Speed-reading is a skill that you can and should learn. Let me give you a simple method here that can double or triple the speed at which you read any book. It's based on the **OPIR** method. These four letters stand for *overview, preview, in view,* and *review.* Here's how you use this technique.

Before you plunge into a book, start with an *overview.* Read the front and back of the book. Read the biography of the author and make sure that this is a person who knows what they are talking about. Read the table of contents and ask yourself whether or not these ideas are of interest to you. Read the appendix and the bibliography quickly to see what information sources the author used. If you get a good feeling about the book, and you think that it has some value for you, go to the next stage.

The second stage of rapid reading is the *preview* stage: take the book and page through it from cover to cover, one page at a time.

Read the chapter headings and paragraph headings. Look at the graphs, charts, and diagrams. Read the first lines of as many paragraphs as you can, and read a couple of paragraphs through to get a feeling for the style of the author. Determine whether or not you are comfortable with the book and whether or not you enjoy the way the author expresses himself. One of the best of all time savers is to decide in advance that the book is not of sufficient value for you to spend several hours reading it.

If after the overview and the preview, you want to read the book, ask yourself, why? This question forces you to think about what you can gain from the book and how you can apply it to your life. This is called *reading on purpose*. The more relevant and applicable the information is, the more likely you are to remember it when you're finished.

The third stage of reading is the *in view*. If you're reading a nonfiction book, start with the chapter that is most interesting to you, and stop if you don't feel like proceeding. Sometimes even an excellent book will have only one or two chapters that are relevant to you right now. If the information is not immediately helpful to you, you'll forget it anyway, so why read it in the first place? As you proceed with the in view, make as many notations as possible, underline key sentences and phrases, and use exclamation points, stars, and quotation marks in the margins. Circle key ideas; make it easy to come back and find the facts that you thought most important.

The final stage of the OPIR method is to *review* the book. No matter how smart you are, you have to go over key points three or four times before they stick in your memory. But once you've marked up a book properly, you can flip through it quickly in as little as an hour and get its entire essence.

How to Find the Best Books

Where do you get the best business books? It's simple. Join one of the business book clubs advertised in the business magazines, get the for free books that they offer at a reduced rate, and add to your library by buying one or two of their choices each year. In no time at all, you will be one of the best-informed people in your circle.

You can also subscribe to Soundview Executive Book Summaries. This is an organization that summarizes two or more taught business books every month. They hire professionals who condense the key points of the book into an easily readable four-to-eight-page format. You can keep abreast of the best that is being written for businesspeople by getting a key synopsis of these books each month. I've gotten a lot of great ideas from these summaries without having to read the entire books.

In expanding your current knowledge, it's important to sub-scribe to the key magazines and publications in your field. If you're in business, you should subscribe to *Fortune* and *Forbes*. If you're in sales, you should subscribe to *Success, Selling,* and *Personal Selling* magazines. If you're in senior management, you should be taking the *Harvard Business Review* and perhaps the *MIT Sloan Management Review.*

The best way to find out what to read is to ask the most success-ful people in your field. What books would they most recommend? What magazines do they enjoy and read the most regularly? By the law of cause and effect, if you read what the best people read, you will soon know what the best people know, and you will develop a winning edge in your field.

The best way to find out what to read is to ask the most successful people in your field.

With magazines, use the rip and read method to save time. Go to the table of contents and circle the articles that you feel would be important to you. Go straight to those articles and tear them out. Throw the rest of the magazine away. Put the torn-out articles into a file, and put it in the back of your briefcase. Whenever you have a few moments, pull out your file and go through the articles with a red pen or a highlighter.

There are two types of reading: maintenance reading and growth reading. Maintenance reading consists of the publications that keep you up-to-date with your field. Growth reading, on the other hand, are the books that increase your knowledge and understanding in your field. They enable you to grow rather than just to stay even.

Audio Learning

Listen to audio learning programs in your car and when you're exercising. The average car owner in America drives 12,000 to 25,000 miles each year. This is the equivalent of 500 to 1,000 hours that you spend in your car each year. Use this time well. Turn your car into a learning machine, a university on wheels. When you're traveling during the daytime, you are not on vacation. You don't have the luxury of driving around listening to the radio or music; this is working time. You must keep your mind fully engaged by continually bombarding it with new ideas and concepts.

You can get the equivalent of three to six months of forty-hour weeks, or one to two full-time university semesters each year, just by listening to audio programs in your car. You can become one of the smartest and highest-paid people in your field by using audio listening to its fullest advantage.

To expand your knowledge, take every seminar and course that you can. Remember, the loser always asks, "How much does it cost?" But the winner always asks, "How much is it worth?" Go to courses taught by practical authorities, by experts. Take courses taught by people who are out there practicing in their fields. Take the courses that are the most relevant and most immediately helpful to you. The faster that you can apply a piece of new information, the more likely you are to learn and retain it for life.

Remember, one good idea is all you need to give yourself an edge in a competitive situation. And the courses and seminars offered today are loaded with good ideas. They're usually taught by highly skilled authorities, who jam a lot of valuable information into a short period of time. Many people I know have doubled and tripled their incomes as a result of attending a single seminar.

One good idea is all you need to give
yourself a competitive edge.

You simply cannot afford to avoid continuous learning. Absorb new ideas like a sponge. Attend trade shows, conventions, and exhibitions, especially those that are relevant to your field. I've spoken at countless annual conventions and association meetings over the years. I have found that the best and highest-paid people in their industries are always at these conventions. They are touring the exhibition floors; they're in the front rows at the key sessions. You must do what the top people do if you want to be one of the top people as well.

Every improvement in your life comes because your mind has collided with a new idea. Your job is to increase the probability of being hit with the right idea at the right time. You do this by deliberately putting yourself into the crossfire of ideas and insights.

Ask for Advice

Finally, one of the most important things you can do to rise to the top of your field in the information age is to ask people for advice and input. Ask them for recommendations for books, audio programs, and courses. Ask them for answers to questions and for solutions to problems. One good piece of advice from someone who's had a similar experience can save you months of hard work and enormous amounts of money.

Benjamin Franklin once said that there are two ways that we can get our knowledge: we can either buy it or we can borrow it. By buying it, we pay full price in terms of time and treasure, but by borrowing it, we get it from others who have already paid full price to learn it. By continually bombarding your mind with new information and ideas, you activate all the mental laws that we've talked about and trigger all the luck factors that we have discussed so far.

Your goal is to become one of the most knowledgeable people in your field. When you do, you will become one of the most valuable and highly paid people in your industry. You will rise rapidly and be promoted steadily. You will move into the top 10 percent of income earners with all the prestige, recognition, and respect that goes with that. You will live in a larger house, drive a newer car, and have a bigger bank account. When people accuse you of being lucky, you can simply tell them, "The more I learn, the luckier I get."

KEYS TO KNOWLEDGE

1. Knowledge determines the quality and quantity of your work and your life.
2. Small differences in knowledge and ability can lead to enormous differences in results.
3. You can learn anything you need to learn to achieve any goal you set.
4. You will never develop a useful talent without, sooner or later, having an opportunity to apply it to some good purpose.
5. Continual reading is the most important way to increase your knowledge.
6. Use the OPIR method for reading: overview, preview, in view, and review.
7. Audio learning, seminars, and courses will supplement your knowledge in important ways.

4

Achievement
and Mastery

You have the ability, right now, to exceed all your previous levels of achievement. You have within you, this very moment, the talents you need to be, have, and do far more than you've ever accomplished in your life. You can learn the skills that you need to achieve any goal that you set for yourself.

> You have the ability, right now, to exceed
> all your previous levels of achievement.

When a virtuoso plays a perfect piece of classical music, or when the Three Tenors—Pavarotti, Domingo, and Carreras—sing exquisite opera, no one ascribes their accomplishments to luck. When a craftsman builds an elegant and refined piece of furniture, no one dismisses his achievement as a matter of good luck.

Whenever you see someone do something in an excellent fashion, you recognize a work of mastery. You know that many weeks, months, and even years of hard work and preparation precede an excellent performance of any kind. My good friend, Nido Qubein, one of the finest professional speakers in America, often invests 100 hours of planning, preparation, and rehearsal for a one-hour talk that he will only give to a single audience on a single occasion. When a professional salesperson carefully analyzes his market, identifies his ideal prospects, sets up and confirm appointments, establishes a high level of rapport, makes an excellent presentation, and walks away with the order, no one can ascribe his accomplishment to luck. In every case, we are talking about mastery.

There is tremendous resentment against achievement in the world today, because in a highly competitive world, it takes many years to become very good at what you do and earn the rewards that go with excellent performance. People who are not willing to put in these efforts resent the rewards that you earn as a result of your dedication. They say you've just been lucky, while they have just been unlucky.

But you know the truth: we live in a universe governed by law, not chaos. There's a reason for everything. Great success is largely the result of higher standards and levels of performance. It's been the same throughout human history, and it is even more true today.

The market only gives extraordinary rewards for extraordinary performance. The market gives ordinary rewards for ordinary performance, and gives below average rewards, unemployment, and insecurity for below average performance.

> The market only gives extraordinary
> rewards for extraordinary performance.

Two Mental Illnesses

Two mental illnesses are rampant today. The first is the "something for nothing" disease, and the second is the "quick fix" disease. Either of these can be fatal to your success, but both of them in combination can be truly disastrous.

The "something for nothing" disease is contracted by people who think that they can get more out than they put in. They think they can put in $1 and get $2 back. They're constantly looking for opportunities to enrich themselves without paying full price. People with this disease are trying to violate the basic laws of the universe: the laws of sowing and reaping, action and reaction, cause and effect. And one of the great success principles is to never attempt to violate universal laws and hope to succeed. Violating universal laws is like attempting to violate the law of gravity.

You've heard the story of the person who jumps off a thirty-story building. As he passes the fifteenth floor, someone leans out of the window and shouts, "How's it going?"

The individual hurling toward the earth shouts back, "So far, so good."

Everyone who is trying to get out more than they put in is in the same situation. They may appear to be doing well in the short term but they are plummeting rapidly toward a rude awakening. Don't let this happen to you.

The second mental illness is the "quick fix" illness. This happens to people who are looking for fast, easy ways to develop key skills that actually require months or years of hard work. Or they're looking for a quick and easy way to solve a problem that may have taken them their whole lives to develop. They become suckers for the latest get-rich-quick scheme. They buy lottery tickets and sign up for pyramid schemes. They buy penny stocks and invest in things that they don't know anything about but promise a quick return. They often waste many years of hard work and savings, searching for the will-o'-the-wisp of quick, easy success.

The law of service says that your rewards will always be equal to the value of your service to others. The universe is always in balance: you will always get out what you put in. If you want to increase the quality and quantity of your rewards, you must focus on increasing the quality and quantity of your service to others.

> Your rewards will always be equal to
> the value of your service to others.

One of the best questions that you can ask yourself every morning is, "How can I increase the value of my service to my customers today?" Your customers are the people who depend upon you for the work you do: the people whose satisfaction determines your rewards, success, recognition, and financial progress.

Who are your customers? If you are working in a job, your boss is your primary customer. Your most important job is to please your boss by doing what he or she considers to be the most important task for you at any given time. If you're a manager, your staff includes your customers. Your job is to please them so that they do an outstanding job to please the people they are meant to serve. If you're in sales or entrepreneurship, the people in the marketplace who use your products or services are perhaps your most important customers. All great fortunes come from providing people with what they want and are willing to pay for better than someone else. It's a truism that you do not get what you want, but what you deserve.

You do not get what you want, but what you deserve.

Your primary job in life is to do whatever is necessary to ensure that you deserve the rewards that you desire. Any attempt to get something that you do not justly deserve is doomed to failure and frustration. All corrupt and criminal activity is aimed at getting rewards without deserving them. The word *deserve* comes from two Latin roots: *de*, meaning *from*, and *servire*, meaning *serve: from service.*

Many people have the uneasy feeling that they do not deserve to be successful and prosperous. They have a fear of success. In fact, you deserve all the good things that life has to offer—as long as you honestly earn them from service to others. Your job is to put in the cause, and the effects will take care of themselves. Your job is to do what you do with excellence, and your rewards will flow to you as the result of law, not by chance or luck.

The great management expert Peter Drucker once wrote that even if you're starting a new business on your kitchen table, your goal must be leadership in your industry, or you shouldn't begin at all. If you merely want to make a quick buck, you will never be successful, and you will probably go broke. But if your goal is to create a business that offers an product or service better than anyone else in a competitive marketplace and you focus on your goal with intensity of purpose, you will achieve an unprecedented success. Like Steve Jobs and Steve Wozniak, designing the first Apple computer in a garage, you can end up building a world-class organization.

Even if you don't build a huge company, your commitment to doing what you do in an outstanding fashion is the greatest single assurance of your success. As an individual, your goal must be to join the top 10 percent of people in your field. Any goal less than being one of the best is not worthy of you. You must be willing to overcome any obstacle, solve any problem, and pay any price to rise into the upper echelons of your work.

Here's a simple test. You can tell if you're in the right field by your attitude toward excellence, especially toward the people at the top. All really successful people have a deep respect and admiration for the highest performers in their industries. Since you always move in the direction of what you most admire, the top people got there by admiring the top people in that field.

Many people today don't particularly care about being at the top. They're content to be way back in the pack, like average run-ners in a marathon race. They're more concerned with security than with achievement. The worst thing is when they go one step further and denigrate successful people. They complain about them behind their backs and point out their faults and shortcom-ings. Alas, this attitude is invariably fatal to success. No one who criticizes the high performers in an industry ever becomes a high performer.

The Law of Practice

The law of practice says that whatever you practice over and over again eventually becomes a new habit or skill. Bear Bryant, the great University of Alabama football coach, once said that success is not a result of the will to win; everyone has that. Great success comes as a result of the willingness to *prepare* to win.

The only real measure of how high you can fly is contained in the question, how badly do you want it? If you want to achieve a level of skill badly enough, and you're willing to pay the price in terms of effort and sacrifice, you will eventually accomplish it. Every extraordinary achievement is the result of thousands of ordinary achievements that no one ever sees or appreciates. Every great accomplishment is the result of hundreds and perhaps thousands of hours of painstaking effort and preparation and study and practice that few people are even aware of. But if you put the effort in, you will eventually get the rewards. When you completely trust this law, it will work for you. The longer you wait, the greater the rewards will be when they come. The poet Henry Wadsworth Longfellow once wrote:

> *The heights by great men reached and kept*
> *Were not attained by sudden flight,*
> *But they, while their companions slept,*
> *Were toiling upward in the night.*

Today successful people are those who were toiling upward in the night while their companions watched television.

Successful people are those who were toiling while their companions watched television.

How can you tell how much preparation you have put in so far? It's easy to measure: just look around you. The laws of sowing and reaping, cause and effect, correspondence, and even mental equivalence all say that your outer world reflects your inner world. Your outer world of accomplishments exactly reflects your inner world of preparation. If you're not happy with your outer world of results and rewards, you have but to go back to work on yourself and change your inner world to make it more consistent with what you want to enjoy on the outside.

The Skills List

Previously I encouraged you to write down ten goals that you want to accomplish in the next twelve months and select the one that would have the greatest positive impact on all your other goals if you were to attain it. This is your major definite purpose.

Now I want you to take this exercise one step further. Once you've decided on the most important goal, ask yourself, "What must I be absolutely excellent at doing in order to achieve this goal?" You can only achieve a goal when you've thoroughly prepared for it. So what skills, abilities, and talents do you need to develop in order to deserve this most important goal?

Just as you need a goals list, you also need a skills list. Make a list of all the skills that you need to enjoy the kind of life that you desire. Skill development comes before the realization of the rewards that you want.

Critical Success Factors

There's an important concept developed at Harvard University called *critical success factors*. These are the skills in which you must be proficient in order to achieve success. In any given field, there are seldom more than five to seven critical success factors, and they can be identified. This is true in sales, management, entrepreneurship, and even parenting. In some cases, there may be only one or two factors that determine the success or failure of the enterprise.

Your most powerful ability is your ability to think. Thomas Edison once wrote that there is no expedient that the average person will not go to, to avoid the hard labor of thinking. To excel in your work, you must think. You must identify the individual components of skill that you will have to master to move to the top.

Here's a great discovery: your weakest critical success factor determines the level at which you can use all your other skills. Let me give you a simple example. If you are excellent in every single aspect of selling except for prospecting, that weakness will set the limit of your success and income. Similarly, if you're excellent at every factor except for closing the sale, that one weakness will determine your level of sales and how much money you make. If you're a manager, and you're excellent at every part of your job except delegating, you will never be successful. That one weakness will hold you back and trip you up every step of the way.

One of the hardest things to do is to admit that you are weak in some area. These areas are often ones that you don't like. Because you don't like them (most salespeople, for example, dislike prospecting), you avoid those areas as much as possible. As a result, your performance gets still weaker. Soon you engage rationalizations and justifications for your poor performance in that area. You blame the marketplace, the products and services, the management, the advertising, and the competition. If you're not careful, you will end up blaming every other force around you except for yourself and your own lack of that skill.

> One of the hardest things to do is to
> admit that you are weak in some area.

What one skill, if you exercised it consistently and in an excellent fashion, would have the greatest impact on your career? You probably knew the answer as soon as you read the question. If you don't know for sure, ask the people around you. Feedback is the breakfast of champions. It's virtually impossible for you to improve without getting candid feedback from others who can view your performance from the outside and tell you what they see. If you're in sales, ask your sales manager. Have them come out with you on sales calls and observe you in action.

We cannot see ourselves as clearly as other people can. If we want to grow, we have to open ourselves up to constructive criticism. Most of us have blind spots that make us impervious to our weaknesses. Sometimes someone will point out a weakness in us, and we will argue angrily with them. We will declare that it's not so; we will insist that we are already good in that area, or at least better than someone else.

But this is not for you. Your goal is to invite constructive feedback so that you can constantly improve. Your goal is to be the best, no matter what the price (especially if the price involves your ego or your pride). Don't let vanity or fragile self-esteem stand in the way of learning what you need to know to move ahead.

Key Result Areas

An extension of critical success factors is *key result areas*. Your key result areas in any position are the specific outcomes or results that you have been hired to achieve. Performance in your key result areas determines your pay, promotion, and prestige. Your ability to identify your key result areas and organize them by priority is essential to achieving mastery. All truly lucky people are very good at doing the one or two things that make all the difference in their work.

A key result area can be defined as a specific outcome for which you are completely responsible. It is measurable, and it is under your control. If you don't do it, it doesn't get done. A key result area is an output of your job and an input for someone else's job. It's an integral part of the function of the organization. For example, if you're in sales, a key result area is closing the sale and getting the check. Once you've done this, the complete order becomes an input for the accounting, manufacturing, distribution, and delivery departments. If you don't do your job, the next steps don't get done. If you do your job well, it influences the behavior and performance of a whole series of other people.

Each key result area has a standard of performance of some kind; it may be vague, or it may be clear. Your job is to set standards of excellence in each of your key result areas. It's therefore essential to be perfectly clear about the most important results that you are expected to contribute to your organization. Then you determine the areas where you must excel in order to perform at your best in those areas.

Another way of defining your key result areas is by asking, what are the specific results for which I am the most highly paid and rewarded? What things do I do that are the most important to the organization? Why exactly am I on the payroll? By defining your key result areas in response to these questions and then organizing them in order of priority from the most important to the least, you now have a track to run on. Your job now is to discipline yourself to become extremely good at doing the one or two things for which you are judged and evaluated the most highly.

Your success in your career will come from excellent performance in the key result areas that are most important to your boss and your company. Your problems in your career will come from inadequate performance in one or more of these areas.

Here's an exercise for you: Write down everything that you believe you've been hired to accomplish. Take this list to your boss, and ask your boss to organize the list by priority. Have your boss tell you what he or she considers to be the most important task. What is the second most important, the third most important, and so on?

From that moment onward, use this list as your operating plan, continually updated in discussion with your boss. Be sure that every minute of every day, you are working on what your boss and your company consider to be the most valuable contribution you can make to the organization. Then commit yourself to doing these tasks very well and better and better.

Incremental Improvement

The law of incremental improvement is a key factor in the luck of all successful people. It says that you get better little by little and bit by bit; excellence is a long, laborious process of tiny, incremental advances, each one of which may be imperceptible, but accumulatively, they add up to mastery of your field.

Excellence is a long, laborious process
of tiny, incremental advances.

When I was growing up, I had low self-esteem and tremendous feelings of inferiority. It never even occurred to me that I could be good at anything. When I saw people who were at the top of their fields, I admired and respected them and simultaneously felt diminished and inferior. I felt that they were somehow of a higher order of being than I was. I concluded that somehow they'd been blessed with intelligence, skills, and abilities that I was lacking. I sold myself short, and I settled for mediocre performance for many years.

Then I had a revelation. It occurred to me that every single person has the ability to be excellent at something, and that excellence was a journey, not a destination. One did not jump from mediocrity to excellence overnight. It was a long, slow process that anyone could embark upon and eventually reach the goal.

Here's the key point: everyone who is at the top in your field was once at the bottom. Everybody who is at the front of the line today was once at the back of the line. Everyone who is at the top of the ladder of success was once at the bottom and climbed up one rung at a time. Remember, it doesn't matter where you're coming from; all that matters is where you're going, and you can learn anything you need to achieve any goal you set for yourself.

In the 1950s and '60s, the Japanese revolutionized their war-torn economy with the *kaizen principle*. The word *kaizen* in Japanese means *continuous betterment*. The French psychologist Émile Coué achieved remarkable cures by teaching people to say, "Every day in every way, I am getting better and better." The Japanese applied the same idea to their industrial enterprises. Every single person in every Japanese company is encouraged to continually look for ideas in their line of sight that can improve the process in some way. In your line of sight, right where you are, you can probably see all kinds of ways to do the job faster and more efficiently. Your job must be to look for and implement new ideas that improve the way things are being done, especially ways customers are being served.

People are not paid high salaries because they are rich; they are paid high salaries because they're highly productive. You attract rewards and riches by being the kind of person who deserves rewards and riches. If you're eventually paid a lot of money for what you do, it will be the direct result of design, not chance. Luck will have nothing to do with it.

Do you want a salary increase? It's easy to get one: just become very good at what you do. The better you get at your job, the more likely your organization is to pay you more to stay with them. And if your current company won't, some other company will come along and offer you more. One of the best ways to get a salary increase is to be hired away by another company because of your reputation for doing an outstanding job. And believe me, everyone knows who the top performers are in every company.

Do you want a salary increase? It's easy to get one:
just become very good at what you do.

I've worked over the years with executive recruiters and personnel consultants. They are continually called upon by companies to find good people. They keep files on the best people in various industries, and they continually upgrade their files. When someone asks them for a top manager, executive, or salesperson, they check their files, and they ask their contacts who the top people are in the current marketplace. Then they go after those people and try to hire them away for their clients by offering them more money.

Sometimes I ask my audiences a painful question: how many of them have been offered a job in the last thirty days? Perhaps 10 or 15 percent of them will raise their hands. I then point out that the top people in every field are continually receiving job offers. It's as though they have set up a force field of magnetism that attracts new and better job opportunities into their lives. Executive recruiters, personnel consultants, and even employers phone them at work, in the evenings, and on the weekends. They're constantly being approached by people who are trying to hire them away by paying them more money and giving them more opportunities.

This is the track that you must be on if you're going to realize your full potential in our competitive economy. The difference between the person who earns $25,000 per year and the person who earns $250,000 per year is not ten times the skill, ability, intelligence, or hours of work. It is often a very marginal difference in performance in the critical success factor areas, which equates to enormous differences in income and rewards.

Here's a question for you: which one would you like to be: the top performer with the high salary, or the low performer with the low salary? This seems to be an obvious question, but it's not. Often when I ask this question, there are looks of confusion on the faces of the audience. They're not sure how to answer. When I ask the question again much louder, everyone wakes up and says they would prefer to be the highest-paid person rather than the lowest-paid person.

The Power of Decision

One great luck factor is contained in the power of decision. People are successful because they have made a clear, unequivocal, door-die decision to be successful. People are unsuccessful because they have never made that decision.

To achieve in your chosen field, you must get serious about yourself and your future. The great majority of people are strolling through life. They want things to get better, and they hope that things will get better, but they have never made a clear, definite, decision to make things better by getting better.

I've spoken to thousands of successful people over the years. For every one of them, the turning point came when they made a clear, written decision to be the best in their fields. As soon as you make that decision, all of the mental laws kick in and begin to work on your behalf. You attract ideas and opportunities for personal and professional improvement. You attract people who can help you with advice and introductions; books, tapes, and articles land on your desk or in your mailbox that help you to become better. You receive seminar and course brochures in the mail. The better you get, the more opportunities you get to use your developing skills and abilities.

One great success factor is love. This principle says that everything you do in life is either to get love or to compensate for the lack of love. A corollary is that you will only be truly successful and happy when you commit yourself wholeheartedly to doing what you most love to do. It's hard for you to have the enthusiasm to begin, and the persistence to continue, on the journey toward excellence unless you really love your chosen field.

You will only be truly successful and happy when you commit yourself wholeheartedly to doing what you most love to do.

If you won $1 million and you could do anything that you wanted, what would it be? In other words, if you had all the time and money that you needed and you were free to choose any occupation, what would you most love to do? All the great successes are men and women who throw their whole hearts into becoming excellent at something they really care about, something they feel makes a difference in the world.

You are engineered in a remarkable way: you will only be truly happy and successful when you feel that you're doing something that benefits other people in some way. This focus on making a difference for others is the common trait of all high-performing, highly paid people in our society.

What kind of a difference do you want to make? Whom do you want to benefit and enrich? How do you want to do it? Which activities give you your greatest feeling of self-esteem and pride? What accomplishments in your past have given you your greatest feeling of importance? What do you enjoy doing more than anything else?

It's been said that life is the study of attention. Your life moves toward the things that most readily attract your attention. One way to tell the right thing to do in the future is by looking at your past. Which skills or abilities have been most responsible for your successes to date? What have you always found it rather easy to do, even though it often came hard to other people? What subjects in school most fascinated you? What activities did you most enjoy? Which part of your current work gives you the most satisfaction? Which activity do you do best? Where do you make the greatest contribution? If you could only do one task all day long from morning to night, which one would you select?

Because the world today is changing rapidly, you are probably going to have a series of jobs and careers over the course of your working lifetime. Every couple of years you will change, either within your organization or from company to company or industry to industry. Your current knowledge and skills will become obsolete, and you'll have to develop new knowledge and new skills in order to remain current.

In fact, a great question for you to ask is, "What is my next job going to be?" Then you can ask, "What is my next career going to be?" And the most important question of all is, "What do I have to be excellent at doing in the future in order to enjoy a high and growing standard of living?"

People who do not plan for the future cannot have one, and the best way to predict your future is to create it for yourself. Since you're going to be changing jobs in the future anyway, you can start right now to define your ideal job. Think through and determine for yourself what you really love to do. You can then develop a plan to become really excellent at this so that you can be paid at the highest levels of your profession. If you don't do this for yourself, no one else is going to do it for you.

People sometimes think it will take them many months or years to achieve mastery in a critical success factor area; consequently, they lose heart and become discouraged before they even begin. But often you can bring up your skill level in a given area in a matter of weeks or even months. Forever afterwards, you will have that skill locked in at a higher level to use in combination with all your other skills. In time you will forget the extra effort and sacrifice that you invested to achieve that level, but you will continue to enjoy the benefits of being one of the best in your field.

The Law of Improvement

The law of improvement states that your life only gets better when you get better. If you want your sales to get better, you must become a better salesperson. If you want your staff to become better, you must become a better manager. If you want your children to become better, you must become a better parent. You can improve any part of your outer world if you improve your skill, ability, or attitude in that area.

Once you've identified the one or two critical skills that you need to develop, write them down as goals. Make a plan for their accomplishment, set a timeline on them, and start to work. Then, no matter how long it takes, just keep on keeping on. Be patient. Rome wasn't built in a day. Important skills take a long time to develop. But if you persevere step by step, you will eventually become one of the best in your field. You will earn the rewards, recognition, and acclaim of the people around you. People will tell you you were lucky to choose that field or commit yourself to excellence in that skill, but you will know that luck had nothing to do with it.

KEYS TO ATTAINING MASTERY

1. Success is the result of higher standards and levels of performance.
2. Every day, ask yourself, "How can I increase the value of my service to my customers today?"
3. Whatever you practice over and over again eventually becomes a new habit or skill.

4. Your outer world of accomplishments reflects your inner world of preparation.

5. Determine the single skill that will have the greatest impact on your career.

6. The turning point in success comes when you make a clear, written decision to be the best in your field.

5

The Power of Personality

Perhaps the most powerful of all luck factors—the one that can make you or break you throughout your life—is the quality of your personality: the attitude that you bring to the world and your relationships.

The law of liking says that the more people like you, the more they will be influenced by you and the more they will help you to achieve your goals. The most popular people tend to be the most successful. A positive mental attitude is closely associated with success in almost everything you do that involves others. When you become a genuinely positive, optimistic person, people will open doors of opportunity for you that would be closed to others. Human beings are predominantly emotional. We decide emotionally and then justify logically. We are almost completely controlled by our feelings, especially in our interactions with others.

The most popular people tend to be the most successful.

You've heard it said that it's not your aptitude, but your attitude that determines your altitude. If you really want to experience a continuous stream of good luck and happy circumstances, you owe it to yourself to develop the kind of attitude that radiates warmth and confidence and attracts people toward you.

The Most Important Word

Earl Nightingale called *attitude* the most important word in the English language. Your attitude is your emotional approach to any person or situation; it's the one thing about you that people are aware of immediately. It radiates from you and your facial expression, your tone of voice, and your body language. The people around you are immediately affected by your attitude and react almost instantaneously. When you're a positive, pleasant, and likable person, people respond by being positive, pleasant, and likable right back. Imagine two salespeople calling on the same business a short time apart. One of them is cheerful, friendly, and pleasant. The other is unsmiling, unhappy, and insecure. Which one is going to get past the gatekeeper and see the prospective customer?

If you have a choice of doing business with two different people, which one would you choose, the positive person or the negative person? The ability to get along well with others, to cooperate and be a good team player, is one of the most valued characteristics in the workplace. Study after study has demonstrated that people are let go more for their inability to get along with others than for any other reason. In times of recession, the negative people are laid off first. The positive people, the ones who get along well with everyone, are always the last to go, if they go at all. If for any reason they are laid off, they're always the first to be hired, either by their previous employer or by someone else.

One way to assure that you have a great life is to be liked and appreciated by everyone you work with. You will get more opportunities, better leads, and steadier promotions. As a result of your positive mental attitude, you will be paid more and given greater responsibilities. People around, above, and below you will want you to succeed and will do everything possible to help you. A person with a positive attitude can make more progress in a couple of years than one with a negative attitude could make in ten years or twenty years. We all like to buy from and work with people who are pleasant, and who make us feel good when we're around them. Perhaps the most important thing you can ever do is to take full control of your thoughts and feelings and make sure they are consistent with the kind of person you want to be.

The law of self-esteem says that the more you like, respect, and appreciate yourself, the more you will like, respect, and appreciate others, and the more they will like, respect, and appreciate you. This is a corollary of the law of correspondence, which says that your outer world will reflect your inner world.

Mental fitness is very much like physical fitness: you can become mentally fit by working out with your mind every single day, just as you become physically fit by working out in a gym on a regular basis. You build your levels of self-esteem, self-confidence, and a positive personality by programming yourself for success. Just as you eat nutritious foods every day to sustain high levels of physical health and energy, you feed your mind with healthy mental foods every day to keep yourself cheerful, optimistic, and upbeat, no matter what happens to you.

The Mental Fitness Program

I've already discussed many of the ingredients in your mental fitness programs. Let's go over some of them one more time. First, to eliminate the negative emotions of anger, blame, envy, resentment, and self-pity, you consciously decide to accept complete responsibility for everything you are and will be. You refuse to make excuses or blame anyone else for anything. You see yourself as the primary creative force in your own life. You realize that you are where you are and what you are because of your own choices and decisions in the past. Since you have made those choices and decisions, you alone are responsible.

You take charge of your entire future by seeing yourself as a creative agent, as a master of change rather than a victim. You never complain and you never explain. If you're not happy with some part of your life, you get busy and do something about it. You refuse to allow negative emotions to interfere with your personality or cloud your vision. You have clear, specific, written goals in each important area of your life. You've created written plans of action to achieve your goals. You work on your major goals every single day. You have a tremendous feeling of forward momentum and progress that fills you with energy, enthusiasm, and excitement. You are so busy working on things that are important to you that you don't have time to worry about the things in your life that may not be perfect. The combination of accepting complete responsibility and designing a clear written plan for your life gives you a foundation upon which you can build as high as you want to go.

You take charge of your future by seeing
yourself as a master of change.

You recognize that knowledge and skill are the keys to the future. The more you learn, the more you earn. The more you know about your chosen field, the more opportunities you have to use your increasing knowledge. You recognize that mastery in your field is absolutely essential to success, achievement, and what people call luck. You have a plan for personal and professional development that includes reading, listening to audio programs, attending seminars, and taking every opportunity to expand your level of knowledge, awareness, and ability. The more you work on becoming better and better at what you need to do to achieve your goals, the more powerful and positive you feel. You know that success is not an accident and that luck is just a way that people explain the good things that happen to people who are good at what they do. You are determined to continually think about the things that you want and keep your mind off of the things that you don't want.

Positive Programming Techniques

To build up your positive attitude, there are a series of powerful, proven mental programming techniques that you can use throughout the day. The first of these is based on the law of affirmation: whatever strong, affirmative statements you repeat over and over in your conscious mind will soon be accepted as commands by your subconscious mind. By the law of subconscious activity, you know that whatever is accepted by your subconscious mind begins to materialize in the world around you. Your reticular activating system increases your awareness and sensitivity to people, ideas, and opportunities that can help you to accelerate your own potential and move more rapidly towards your goals. Fully 95 percent of your emotions are determined by the way that you talk to yourself. Psychologist Martin Seligman calls this your *explanatory style*. The way that you talk to yourself and explain things to yourself largely determines how you feel about your world and what is going on around you.

If you don't consciously and deliberately think and talk about the things you want, your mind will unfortunately slip toward thinking about the things that you worry about and make you upset or angry. You must firmly grasp the steering wheel of your life and keep your thoughts focused on where you're going, or you will end up in a ditch of depression and negativity. Positive self-talk and positive affirmations are the key. With positive affirmations, your potential is unlimited. You can literally talk yourself into becoming the kind of person that you want to be so you can achieve the goals you've set for yourself.

You can build your self-esteem by continually repeating the words, *I like myself, I like myself, I like myself* over and over. When you first say, *I like myself,* you may feel a little funny inside. This is to be expected. Psychologists call it *cognitive dissonance.* It happens when a new positive message clashes against an old, negative message that you may have accepted in the past as a result of earlier experiences. But when you repeat the positive affirmation *I like myself* over and over, eventually your subconscious mind accepts that you do genuinely like yourself and alters your personality accordingly. The more you like yourself, the more you like others, and the more you like others, the more they like you and want to cooperate with you.

Build your self-esteem by repeating the words, *I like myself, I like myself, I like myself* over and over.

But it begins with you. Say to yourself over and over again, *I'm the best, I'm the best, I'm the best.* Whenever you think of yourself and your work, tell yourself in strong, positive language that you are the best. Again, you may feel a little bit silly at first, but after a while it will feel better and better. Start off every day by saying *I feel happy, I feel healthy, I feel terrific.* When people ask you how things are going, always reply positively: say, "Great" or "Things are going wonderfully." Talk about yourself and your life the way you want them to be, not the way they might happen to be at the moment.

Remember, your subconscious mind, which controls your attitude, personality, body language, emotions, and levels of enthusiasm, excitement, and energy, has no capacity to think or decide by itself. It merely accepts instructions. Your conscious mind is the gardener, and the subconscious is the garden. You can plant either flowers or weeds; either will grow. But if you don't deliberately plant flowers, your garden will fill up with weeds by default.

The Law of Substitution

One of the most powerful of all luck factors is the law of substitution. Many people have told me that understanding this simple principle has changed their lives. The law of substitution says that your conscious mind can only hold one thought at a time, and you can choose that thought. You can substitute a positive thought for a negative thought anytime you choose, and you are always free to choose the way you think or feel at any time. The way you act or react is a result of a choice that you have decided to make, either consciously or unconsciously. If you're happy or unhappy, angry or exhilarated, enthusiastic or depressed, in every case, you've decided to feel this way. It's always a matter of choice, and the choice is always up to you. By using positive affirmations, you can keep your mind centered on positive messages that are life-enhancing and improve your attitude toward yourself and others.

You can also use the law of substitution to block out negative thoughts by instead thinking about your goals. Life is a continuous succession of problems. At this very moment, your life is filled with problems of all kinds, large and small, and if you don't watch out, they will surge in, fill your mind, and preoccupy you. The more you think about your problems, the more negative, depressed, and angry you will become.

You can counter this tendency by thinking about your goals. Whenever something makes you angry, neutralize the negative thought by thinking about your goal. Repeat it in the form of a personal, present-tense affirmation. Talk to yourself about what you want. Use that to keep your mind off the things that you don't want.

Another tremendous way to use the law of substitution is by thinking about the future rather than the past. Whenever you have a problem, discipline yourself to stop rehashing it and who was to blame. Instead, think about the solution and what you are going to do next. The instant that you begin thinking in terms of solutions and future actions, your mind becomes calm, clear, and positive. Almost all negativity refers to past events or circumstances. Positive thinking comes from thinking about your goals and the specific, concrete, positive things that you could be doing right now to move toward them more rapidly.

Think about the future rather than the past.

Another valuable antidote to worry or negativity is to get so busy working on something that's important to you that you don't have time to think about anything except where you're going in life.

Positive Visualization

Another key part of mental programming is positive visualization: feeding your mind with a continuous stream of positive images that are consistent with the person you want to be and the life you want to live. All improvement in life begins with an improvement in your mental pictures. If you talk to unhappy people and ask them what they think about most of the time, you won't be surprised to find that they think about their problems, their bills, their negative relationships, and all the setbacks and obstacles in their lives. But when you talk to successful, happy people, you find that they spend most of their time thinking about the things that they want to be and have and do. Your mental pictures are like your affirmations. They are accepted by your subconscious mind as commands, and it goes to work to bring them into your reality.

In the morning, people often think about how much money they want to earn. In the afternoon, they think about their financial problems. In the evening, they go home and worry about their bills. They keep sending their minds a series of conflicting and contradictory messages. It's like giving a taxi driver different instructions at every corner: they never get anywhere. Luck requires fully activating the law of attraction and drawing into your life, from all directions, people and circumstances that can help you to move ahead. By thinking about what you want and keeping your mind off what you don't want, you tend to be luckier and luckier in everything you attempt.

Over the years, I've found it helpful to buy magazines full of pictures of the things that I've wanted. When my wife and I were talking about the kind of house we wanted to live in, we bought every magazine that described beautiful homes. We went out on weekends and visited beautiful homes in expensive neighborhoods. We would walk through open houses from one end to the other, thinking about the features that we liked. We continually discussed what our dream house would look like. We made careful lists and gave a lot of consideration to our needs, both in the present and in the future. And it wasn't very long before we found a house that was perfect for us in every respect. That wasn't luck.

Perhaps the most important ingredient that you can add to the process of affirmation and visualization is the constant emotionalization of your words and mental pictures. The luck formula says that thought times emotion equals reality. The more that you can emotionalize a goal, an affirmation, or a picture, the more energy it has, and the more rapidly it is acted upon by your subconscious mind. When you have an intense, burning desire for achievement, you generate excitement and enthusiasm that drive you forward and over any obstacles. The more you really want something, and the more you affirm and visualize it, sending it from your conscious to your subconscious mind, the more energy and power you have. Good things happen to you that other people describe as luck.

Thought times emotion equals reality.

The Law of Reversibility

The law of reversibility has been with us for thousands of years, and it's been taught by many of the great teachers throughout history. William James of Harvard rediscovered it in 1905. This law says that just as feelings generate actions that are consistent with them, actions generate feelings that are consistent with them. This means that you can act your way into feeling the way you want to feel. You can program your subconscious mind by pretending that you already have the qualities and characteristics that you most desire.

For example, you may wake up in the morning not feeling positive and enthusiastic about the day; you may feel reluctant to call on new customers or visit your banker. But if you deliberately pretend as though you are positive and confident in every respect, after a few short minutes you will start to feel that way: you will feel happy and in control, optimistic and outgoing; your actions will create the feelings or emotions that are consistent with them.

How many times does the football team that is behind in the second quarter get a pep talk from the coach in the locker room? After that, the team goes charging out onto the field as though they could conquer the world. Very often this new enthusiasm turns the game around and takes them to victory.

You can become your own cheerleader by talking to yourself positively and then acting as if you are already the person that you wanted to be. Fake it until you make it. Act as though you are trying out for the role of an outstanding, positive, warm, cheerful, happy, and likable person. Walk, talk, act, and behave as if you were already that person—as though you had just won an award for being the best person in your industry. The more you act the part, the more you program these behaviors and attitudes into your subconscious mind, where they lock in permanently.

Empathy and Emotional Reciprocity

Another great luck factor is empathy. Stephen Covey, author of *The Seven Habits of Highly Successful People*, says, seek first to understand, then to be understood. One of the fastest ways to overcome shyness and insecurity around others is to become more involved with them. Ask questions and listen intently to the answers. Most people are so preoccupied with themselves that they pay little attention to anyone else. But when you empathize with others by asking them questions and listening to them when they talk, they will like you, they will want to cooperate with you, and your own shyness will disappear.

Seek first to understand, then to be understood.

An extension of the principle of empathy is the law of emotional reciprocity: when you do and say things that make other people feel good, they will have an unconscious desire to pay you back and to make you feel good as well. My late friend Cavett Robert, the great professional speaker, used to tell how as a young man, he used to run out onto the stage and say to himself, "Here I am." As he matured, his attitude toward his audience changed completely: now he would walk out onto the stage and say to himself, "There you are."

What do people really want with regard to emotional reciprocity and empathy? Since you are a person as well, you have inside knowledge of how to be a great success in your interactions.

What you want—and what other people want—is to feel important. You want to feel valued, appreciated, and worthwhile. You want people to like you, respect you, and treat you nicely. You want people to do things that raise your self-esteem and cause you to like and respect yourself even more. The people that you like the most are the ones who make you feel the best about yourself. This is the key to excellent human relationships. With every person you meet, look for something you can say that will make that person feel better about himself or herself. At the very least, never condemn, complain, or criticize. If you can't say anything nice, don't say anything at all. Even if you have a problem or criticism, it's better to start off by asking for help and taking the low road in the conversation.

When you look for ways to satisfy the deep, subconscious needs of others for appreciation, admiration, and attention, they will be unconsciously motivated to help you to achieve your goals as well. Get out of your own way. Stop thinking about yourself; instead think about how you can make other people feel better about themselves.

The Power of Image

There's another key element of luck and success that is overlooked by most people. It is image: how you appear to others in your day-to-day interactions. Sometimes your image can make or break you in a critical relationship. People are highly visual. You've heard it said that you never get a second chance to make a good first impression. We meet so many people under so many circumstances that we are constantly judging and sorting. This process takes place unconsciously. We're not even aware of it. But often we make an instant decision about a person that sticks for the rest of the time we know that person.

Research shows that people make up their minds about you in the first four seconds. Each person's mind is like quick-drying concrete, and the first four seconds leaves the first impression. The cement sets in thirty seconds. After that, the person will look for things to justify their initial impression. Because of the way the human mind is constructed, people use selective perception. They will ignore or reject things that are inconsistent with what they have already decided to believe.

People make up their minds about you
in the first four seconds.

The most successful people at every level of society are those who look the best on the outside. They don't leave their first, or second, impressions to chance. They give a lot of thought to their appearance, they carefully study other successful people, and they dress accordingly. They constantly observe the top people in their fields, and they strive to look like them.

Rightly or wrongly, you deal with other people based on your perception of them. Your initial perception is formed at the moment of first meeting the person. First impressions make the greatest impact. It's not that your assessment of the person won't change over time: this does happen, but it is rare. Once the impression is made, it becomes your sense of the reality of the individual.

You've heard it said that birds of a feather flock together, or like attracts like. As you rise to higher levels in your business and personal life, you will find that the people at each higher level dress better than people at the lower levels. Successful people can recognize other successful people across a crowded room. Just as birds have plumage that enables them to be recognized by other birds of the same kind, individuals have plumage in the form of the clothes they wear, their grooming, and their accessories. Because of the law of attraction, people who look similar seem to be attracted to each other in social and business situations.

You are most comfortable dealing with people who are very much like you; so is everyone else. If you want powerful, important people to be comfortable dealing with you, you must dress the way they dress and carry yourself the way they carry themselves. The ideal business colors for men are navy blue and dark gray. These are also the ideal colors for women (in addition, women can wear hunter green). Men should wear white shirts and silk ties carefully coordinated with the color of their suits. Women should wear accessories that complement the color and design of their clothes. Both men and women should wear high-quality shoes, properly polished.

There's an acceptable level of grooming for both men and women at every level of society. If a man wants to drive a truck, he can wear a beard with hair down his back. If he wants to be successful in business, he should have a conservative hairstyle and a clean-shaven face. I remember a young man working in sales who was doing very poorly. He had the right education, the right clothes, the right personality, and the right energy level, but he was having no luck with his sales. Both he and his boss were extremely frustrated, and his boss was thinking of letting him go.

The young man had a full beard and a mustache. He thought it was clever and different. But interviews with customers demonstrated that facial hair, especially a beard, denotes a person who is eccentric or even untrustworthy. When the young man learned this, he went home and shaved off his beard and mustache. His sales results changed overnight. Within two months, he was the top salesman in the company. The same people that were reluctant to talk to him were suddenly his best customers and were referring him to other people. He told me that if he had not learned about how improper grooming, especially facial hair on a man, could hold a person back, he would probably have failed in his new career.

One of the great principles of luck is this: everything counts. Every little thing that you do, or don't do, counts in some way. Everything helps or hurts. Everything adds or takes away. Everything moves you toward your goals or moves you away from them. You've heard it said that the devil is in the details. This is as true for your image as it is for any other part of your life. Little things do mean a lot.

I suggest that you read at least one book on how to dress for success. Leave nothing to chance. Study the top people around you. If you work for a salary, dress the way that people two jobs above you dress; spend twice as much on your clothes, and buy half as many. If you're a junior clerk, come to the office looking like a junior executive, and you will immediately attract the attention of people who can help you. If you combine an excellent professional image with a commitment to continuous growth, knowledge, and skill, you will put yourself onto the fast track, and the people who can help you the most will be the ones opening the most doors for you.

Image is so important because when you look excellent, you feel excellent as well. When you look around you and you know that you are one of the best-dressed people in the room, you have a tremendous feeling of pride, confidence, and self-esteem. You like and respect yourself even more. As a result, you like and respect others, and you are more sensitive, courteous, and gracious in your relationships with them. When you dress like a winner, you think and feel like a winner.

By the law of reversibility, your outer actions of walking, talking, acting, grooming, and behaving like an outstanding individual have a backflow effect: they will make you feel like an outstanding individual in everything you do. And remember, everything counts.

Your personality and attitude are perhaps the most powerful of all luck factors. When you combine them with a commitment to excellence, you trigger the desire of people around you to help you to move forward. The nicer you are to others, the nicer they will be to you. The more positive you are, the more people will want to be involved with you and do business with you.

Leadership, especially personal leadership, only takes place when people want you to be the leader. The better you are at cooperating and interacting with others, the more they will want you to be successful. They will look for ways to help you to achieve your goals. And luck will have nothing to do with it.

KEYS TO IMPROVING YOUR PERSONALITY AND ATTITUDE

1. The more you like yourself, the more you will like others, and the more they will like you.

2. Whatever strong, affirmative statements you repeat over and over in your conscious mind will soon be accepted as commands by your subconscious mind.

3. Whatever is accepted by your subconscious mind begins to materialize in the world around you.

4. You can substitute a positive thought for a negative thought anytime you choose.

5. You can improve your life by consciously creating positive mental pictures and generating a burning, intense desire for them.

6. Empathy is the most important way to get others to like you.

7. The most successful people are those who look the best on the outside.

6

Expanding Your Network

In the previous chapter, I gave you some ideas for becoming a more positive, optimistic, and likable person. In this chapter, you will learn how to expand your network of contacts and relationships in order to increase the likelihood of meeting the right person at the right time with the right information or opportunities for you.

The law of relationships says that the more people who know you and think of you in a positive way, the more success and opportunity you will have. Every change in your life will involve other people. If you wish to achieve big goals, you need the active involvement and cooperation of many different people. Over the years, your life has been affected and your life direction has been changed by a simple comment, a piece of advice, or an action by a particular person at a particular time.

A friend of mine was building his business in an extremely competitive market. He needed more money to expand. He began calling on local banks with his business plan. One by one, they turned him down and told him that his business would never be successful. But he was an optimist, so he drew a series of ever expanding concentric circles on a map around the address of his business and began calling on banks at ever greater distances. Finally, he found a banker ninety-five miles away who liked his business plan and lent him the money he needed. He is today one of the wealthiest and most successful entrepreneurs in America.

I asked him if he had ever thought about giving up in his search for more money. He said, "Absolutely not. I knew that I would eventually get the money if I spoke to enough people. I was prepared to visit banks even 500 miles from my office if that was what it took to find the right banker with the right attitude." This is a key luck factor and an important part of success. The law of probability says the more different things you try, the more likely you are to try the right thing at the right time.

> The more different things you try, the more likely
> you are to try the right thing at the right time.

The more people you know, and the more consistently you expand your range of contacts, the more likely you are to meet the person you need at exactly the right time, with exactly the right resources for you. It is no miracle, and it has nothing to do with luck. The most successful people are those who know, and are known by, the greatest number of other successful people. Do people become successful and then meet other successful people? Or do they meet these people and then become successful themselves? It can work either way. Many people make the mistake of thinking that by seeking out successful people, they will be able to piggyback on their knowledge, advice, and resources. But this will only work for a short time. In the long run, you can never get and hold on to anything to which you are not entitled as the result of your own consciousness.

The law of attraction is the most vital of all the luck factors. You inevitably attract into your life the people and circumstances that are in harmony with your dominant thoughts. The opposite of the law of attraction is the law of repulsion: you automatically repel people and circumstances that are not in harmony with your dominant thoughts. When you are a completely positive thinker, you set up a force field of energy that attracts positive people and situations. If you're a negative thinker, you set up a field of negative energy that drives these forces away.

Many people have transformed their lives in as little as a day simply by taking full control over their minds and disciplining themselves to think and talk only about the things they want and the direction they are going in. Again, the act of writing down clear, specific goals, making plans for their accomplishment, and working on them every single day will change your thinking. It will also change the force field of energy around you almost instantly.

The Law of Indirect Effort

Birds of a feather do flock together. People at similar levels of success tend to be attracted to one another, and you cannot fake it for very long. This brings us to another important luck factor: the law of indirect effort. It says that you get what you want with other people more often indirectly than directly. In fact, if you attempt to get other people to help you or cooperate with you directly, you'll often end up looking foolish and even drive those people away. But if you're using the law of indirect effort, you will be amazed at how successful you can be.

For example, if you want to have more friends, how do you use the law of indirect effort? It's simple. Concentrate on being a good friend to other people. Take an interest in other people. Ask them questions and listen to their answers. Practice empathy: be concerned about their problems and their situations. Look for ways to help them, even if it's just being a friendly sounding board. The more you concentrate on being a good friend, the more friends you will have. You will attract people into your life like bees to honey.

Do you want to impress other people? The worst way to do it is the direct way: by trying to impress them. The best way is the indirect way: by being impressed by other people. The more impressed you are with other people and their accomplishments, the more impressed they will be by you.

When you meet a new person, remember that everyone has done something that is noteworthy and impressive. Your job is to find it out. Ask people what they do, how they got into that particular field, how everything's going. If you listen carefully, people will tell you about both their successes and their problems. When a person mentions that they have just achieved something worthwhile, nod, smile, and congratulate them for their success. Everybody loves a compliment.

A successful businessman I know made a habit of sending ten telegrams every week to people he had met. The telegrams contained a single word: "Congratulations." Over the years, he built up a network of men and women who liked and respected him. They were amazed that he had known that they had accomplished something worthwhile. Later on in life, when he was asked how he managed to be aware of the accomplishments of his friends, he said that he had no idea what they were doing. He just knew that everybody is accomplishing something every day and every week. When you send them a message of congratulations, they will automatically apply that message to the situation that has just worked out successfully for them.

Using the law of indirect effort, you constantly look for ways to compliment and congratulate people on what they're doing, what they have accomplished, how they're dressed, recent decisions they have made, or even the fact that they have lost a few pounds. In our society, one of the best compliments that you can give to anyone is, "You look like you've lost weight." Even if it's not true, people always enjoy that someone has noticed (rightly or wrongly) that they have lost weight. Why? Because everyone wants to be physically attractive, and physical attractiveness is closely associated with being thin, trim, and fit. You can never go wrong by complimenting somebody on how good they look.

Constantly look for ways to compliment
and congratulate people.

Do you want people to respect you? This is one of the deepest subconscious needs that we all have. They say that babies cry for it and grown men die for it. Almost everything you do is to earn (or at least not to lose) the respect of people you respect. If you want people to respect you, respect them in advance. We've moved away from the era of the go-getter: we are now in the era of the go-giver. The great majority of underachievers are those who are trying to get something out before they put something in, but this is not for you. You know the law of sowing and reaping. You know that you get out what you put in. You also know that you cannot reap until you have sown. Concentrate on sowing good thoughts, good ideas, and good feelings in your relationships. And you know that, as a matter of universal law, it will all come back to you in the most remarkable ways.

The Law of Giving

The law of giving says that the more you give of yourself without expectation of return, the more will come back to you from the most unexpected sources. Many people make the mistake of thinking their good should come back from the people they have been good to, but this seldom happens. When you give of yourself freely and openly to someone else—either of your time, your money, or your emotions—that person will rarely be the one who repays you in kind. Instead, you will be activating one of the greatest laws of the universe: the law of attraction. Powers will be put in motion that will bring you the good that you need and desire, usually from a completely different source, but at exactly the right time and place for you.

Why should this happen? It's easy to understand. When you do something nice for another person, it raises your own self-esteem and makes you feel terrific about yourself. There is something about giving of yourself to others that makes you glow as a person. You are engineered in such a way that you can only be truly happy when you know you are making a positive difference in the lives of others. In fact, you benefit as much as, and often much more than, the person for whom you do a kindness. You change the force field of mental energy around you. By helping others, you intensify the power of attraction and draw into your life happy people and circumstances, from sources that you could not imagine or predict.

For example, imagine you are driving from point A to point B to meet a sales prospect. You're in a hurry, but you see an old person stopped by the side of the road with a flat tire. Even though you're on a tight schedule, you overcome your impatience; you stop and help the person replace their tire. The person offers to pay you, but you refuse. You wish them Godspeed, and you hurry along on your journey. The whole incident takes about ten minutes. Perhaps, unbeknownst to you, you have just activated the powers of the universe in your behalf.

You arrive at your appointment a little late, but you find that the person you're going to meet with is even later than you. Nothing is lost. Not only that, but something has happened. The person you meet with, rather than being reluctant, is very much in need of what you're selling and makes an immediate decision to buy. You walk out with one of the best and easiest orders you've ever gotten. If you're not careful, you start thinking about how lucky you were. But it wasn't luck. It was law.

Generosity of all kinds triggers happy, fortuitous, lucky events in your life. Throughout the ages, men and women have tithed their way to great success and fortune: they have regularly given 10 percent or more of their income to worthy causes. This attitude and action of giving sets up a force field of energy that draws financial opportunities that are far greater than any money they give away.

Generosity triggers lucky events in your life.

When you give generously of yourself, you change your mental space, you shape the inner aspects of your mind. You create a new mental equivalent that is more consistent with the satisfaction, joy, and success that you desire. You become a truly lucky person.

Because relationships are so important, they cannot be left to chance. Most people are like balls banging around on the billiard table of life. They're like bumper car drivers at the fair, colliding randomly, with little control over whom they run into or who runs into them. They live by the law of accident.

This is not for you. Make a specific plan for the relationships you want to develop. Remember, you free yourself from the law of accident by living your life by design. Instead of having things happen to you in a random and haphazard way, you deliberately plan what you want to have happen. The clearer you are about what you want, the more rapidly you attract it into your life and recognize it when it comes.

Finding Your Ideal Mate

Here's a simple example: your choice of a mate in marriage or a key relationship will do more to determine your success and happiness than perhaps any other factor. You know countless people who have worked hard for years to gain material success and then seen it all fall to pieces when their relationships with their spouse and children disintegrated for lack of time and attention.

You find your ideal mate in the same way you achieve any worthwhile goal in life. You sit down with a pad of paper and write out a description of the perfect person for you. As you do, imagine that you are putting in an order that you are going to mail away to the other side of the country, and the perfect person is going to be delivered back to you exactly the way you have described. Write down every detail. Describe the person's appearance, height, weight, and level of physical fitness. Describe the person's temperament, personality, sense of humor, education, intelligence, and attitude. Be as precise as you can about the person's values, beliefs, philosophies, and opinions about the important things in life. The more detailed your description, the better. Read and reread this description every day, adding new details as you think of them. Modify and adjust the description to make it more and more accurate and precise. Each time you review it, you drive it deeper and deeper into your subconscious mind.

When you imagine how happy you will feel when you are in a relationship with the perfect person for you, this emotional component activates your subconscious mind and triggers the law of attraction. In no time at all, you will draw that person into your life.

The next step in finding your ideal relationship is to do an honest evaluation of yourself. A self-actualizing person is objective and frank about his or her strengths and weaknesses. Make a list of everything that you have to offer in a relationship. What are your good points? What characteristics and qualities have you developed over the years that make you a worthwhile catch?

Be honest with yourself: make a list of the areas where you still have work to do. Are you not as disciplined as you would like to be? Do you use your time as well as you would like? Are you sometimes impatient, irritable, or demanding? Write these problem areas down, and work to improve yourself in each of them. You cannot attract into your life a person that is very different from the person you are deep inside. If you want to attract a wonderful mate, you must become a good person yourself. Your relationships, especially your most important ones, will always reflect your true personality, values, beliefs, and attitudes. You will always experience on the outside what you truly are on the inside.

> If you want to attract a wonderful mate,
> you must become a good person yourself.

Attracting Business Relationships

Once you've made some decisions about what you want in your personal life, it's time to decide what kind of relationships you want in your business and career. One secret of success in the law of work is to select your boss carefully. When you look for a job, you are going to be exchanging your life—your most precious possession—for the opportunity to work and get results and the income that goes along with them. The key to your success at work is going to be the quality of your relationship with your boss. Choose your boss with care. Interview carefully until you find the kind of person you would really like to work for. You need someone that you like, respect, admire, and look up to. You want to work for someone who has a lot to teach you and who will encourage and support you in doing the best job you can.

If you're working for a negative boss, or working in a negative situation where you are subjected to continual criticism, you'll never be happy or successful. Eventually you'll quit or be fired. You'll have to find a new job somewhere else working with, and for, different people.

Smart people adamantly refuse to work in a situation that they don't enjoy most of the time. They know that anything else is a waste of time and a waste of life. I've seen countless occasions where a good person has left a negative work environment and joined a company with a positive, optimistic, encouraging boss and a group of great coworkers. In no time at all, the person who was doing poorly in one environment began to thrive and grow in the new one.

Get around the Right People

The most important decision that you make for your success is your choice of the people with whom you habitually associate. Get around the right people. Get around winners, and get away from negative people. Get away from people who complain, condemn, and criticize all the time. These toxic people depress you and take the joy out of living. After you've spent time with them, you feel discouraged and unmotivated. Instead, choose your friends and associates with care. As Baron de Rothschild once said, "Make no useless acquaintances; be perfectly selfish with regard to the people in your environment."

David McClelland's research into achievement at Harvard University demonstrated that after twenty-five years, the members of your reference group will have had more of an impact on your success and happiness than any other choices you make. Your reference group is made up of the people with whom you identify and associate most of the time. If you fly with eagles, you will think and feel like an eagle. If you associate with turkeys, you will think, walk, act, and speak like a turkey. The people around have an inordinate influence on every part of your life and everything you accomplish.

Successful people are often described as loners. This does not mean that they actually are loners. They have good friends and relationships, but they don't go out for lunch with whoever is standing by the door at lunchtime. They are very selective: they spend time only with people they enjoy and whose company they can benefit from. You must do the same.

Self-made millionaires in America are inveterate networkers: they know that the more people they know, and who know them, the more luck they're going to have in making sales and discovering opportunities. They take every opportunity to network with other people and build up a broader network of overlapping contacts.

Self-made millionaires are inveterate networkers.

I have some good friends who once moved to a new city in a new country. Within a few months, they became some of the most active and popular people in their industries. How did they do it? Networking. They immediately got involved in industry associations and organizations. They became fully engaged and contributed wholeheartedly to the organizations' activities. Because only a few people do this, they soon rose to positions of prominence in planning and organizing the major committees and functions. They were soon recognized and respected by all the key people in the industry. They developed a reputation for making a contribution and getting things done, and opportunities and possibilities began to flow their way. They easily gained the support of key people inside and outside of their organizations. They made more progress in a few months than many people had made in several years.

The key to networking is to select one or two organizations that contain people who can be of assistance to you (and whom you can help as well). The law of credibility is a key luck factor. It says that the more people believe and trust you, the easier it is for them to decide to work with you and do business with you.

Build Credibility

Again, everything counts. Everything you do in your relationships either helps or hurts your credibility. One main reason for joining key organizations is to begin building your credibility with the people who can help you in the future.

Here's the formula for successful business networking: When you join an organization, study it carefully. Ask what the organization does and what parts of it are the most active and most important to the organization's success. Study the roster of members and the committee structure. Be sure that you are joining an organization with members that are ahead of you in your career. They must be people that you can learn and gain from, who can pull you up to higher levels than you have attained on your own.

Once you've identified a key committee in an organization, volunteer for it. Since everything that is done in business and social organizations is largely voluntary, your willingness to contribute your time and effort will always be welcome.

Most people who join associations do little more than attend the functions and go home. They look upon the meetings as an extension of their social life rather than as a key part of their business lives. But when you join, you not only volunteer for responsibilities, you become actively involved. You volunteer for more assignments, you put your head down, and you perform whatever tasks are given to you. You attend every meeting and you contribute to every discussion. You do your homework before and after the meeting so that you are thoroughly prepared. In no time at all, the key people will take notice of you. By constantly giving of yourself with no expectation of return, you will begin to earn their respect and trust. Your credibility with them will increase; their confidence in your ability to perform ever more complex tasks will go up. You will soon become a key player on the committee and a valuable member of the organization.

Getting Involved

Some years ago, I joined the Chamber of Commerce for the express purpose of getting involved in the business community and making a contribution of some kind. I found that the key issue that the Chamber was involved in at that time was the business education. I volunteered for the business education committee, which liaised with the government. I put in a good number of hours doing research and writing papers for the committee. I attended every meeting; I suggested different strategies and tactics that the committee could use to be a more active player with the government in increasing the quality of education in the state.

In no time at all, I was the vice chairman of the committee. I assigned all of the Chamber's major responsibilities in that area. The chairman of the committee was one of the senior business-men in the community. He was extremely powerful and linked to a variety of businesses and government organizations. I worked under him and followed his guidance and instruction. He opened doors for me and introduced me to other key businesspeople, who could give me input and advice on the Chamber's business and education activities.

Six months later, the annual meeting of the Chamber, attended by several hundred delegates—every one of them leading businesspeople—was held in a resort. They asked me if I would prepare the agenda of speakers and emcee the meeting.

Again, I accepted with enthusiasm. I spent many hours preparing and studying backgrounds of the speakers. At the meeting, I was front and center as the emcee and chairman for the entire day, in front of hundreds of top business delegates. Because I had done my homework, I was thoroughly prepared to do the job in a competent manner.

In the next year, I was chairing meetings between groups of senior business executives and senior government officials. Some of these meetings were written up in the newspapers, including comments that I had made and that politicians had made in response.

Another major businessman read the comments and decided that he wanted me to run one of his businesses. I was hired away from my current job at double the salary, plus stock options. Before the dust had settled, I was one of the best-known and respected young businessmen in the state. I was on a first-name basis with senior politicians, top businesspeople, and the heads of several private and public organizations.

I was invited to become a key player with the United Way in their annual fundraising drive. This brought me to the attention of still more senior businesspeople and gave me even more opportunities to expand my contacts.

In another couple of years, my income doubled again. There seemed to be a direct relationship between the ever-widening circle of contacts I was forming and the opportunities that I had to work, invest, travel, and interact with key people.

My story is not unique. Countless people have had the same experience, but it depends on you. It's up to you to get out there and get involved. There are always vastly more opportunities to serve the community and social, business, or charitable organizations than there ever will be talented people to fill those slots. There are no limits to the degree to which you can expand your contacts if you approach the situation as a giver rather than a taker.

The Law of Indirect Effort

When you meet a new person you feel would be valuable for you to know, remember the old saying: he who asks questions has control. Use the law of indirect effort. Instead of trying to impress the other person, ask questions and be impressed by what he or she says to you. Look for opportunities to help—to put in rather than to take out. Remember, the principle of sowing and reaping is universal. If you put in long enough and hard enough, you will eventually get out all that you could possibly want.

Every businessperson that you meet is concerned and preoccupied about his or her business. Here's a great question for you to ask each person: what do I have to know about your business to recommend you to a prospective customer client? People love to talk about what they do and why other companies patronize them or should patronize them. And there is nothing that will build a faster bond between you and another businessperson than by your recommending a customer or client to that person. When you help other people build their businesses and achieve their goals, they will be predisposed to helping you improve your business as well.

The Law of Liking

Another way of stating the law of liking is that the more a person likes you, the easier it is to influence that person. Emotions distort valuations. If a person really likes you, he or she will be less concerned about any shortcomings you might have. On the other hand, if a person dislikes you, he or she will be hypersensitive to your shortcomings. People like to do business with people they like. People like to socialize with people they like. People like to open doors for people they like. People like to buy from people they like. People like to hire and promote people they like. The more people like you, the more opportunities will open up for you, and the faster you will move ahead in your career. Continually offer to help the people you meet.

The more a person likes you, the easier
it is to influence that person.

I've seen some of the wealthiest and most powerful business-people in the world in action. I have always been amazed to notice how courteous and attentive they are when they're listening to others. Almost invariably they ask, "Is there any way I can help you?" In any conversation, with anyone, ask that same question. Sometimes the person will think of something that you can do; in most cases, not. But your active offer to help will leave a pleasant memory in their mind, and, sometime down the line, they may call on you for help.

The law of reciprocity is one of the most powerful of all princi-ples. It simply says that if you do something for another person, the other person will want to do something for you. They will want to reciprocate in some way so they don't feel under obligated to you. Most human beings are extremely fair, and they want to stay even in their lives. When you do something nice for another person, they will instinctively want to "get even" with you by doing something nice for you as well. If you go out for lunch with a friend and you pick up the tab, he or she will insist on picking it up next time. If you invite a friend over to your home for dinner, he or she will insist on inviting you over at another time. When you send a Christmas card to someone, they will send a Christmas card back, even if they don't know you.

When you organize your life in harmony with universal laws, you will be astonished at the speed at which good things start to happen for you. The law of reciprocity in human relationships is one of the most powerful principles you will ever learn. The key to success is to build more and better relationships, for you to become more known and respected by a greater circle of people. Do this deliberately and consciously, selecting the people in organizations you want to be associated with and then throwing your whole heart into contributing to those people and organizations.

Human beings always seek to follow the line of least resistance. The line of least resistance in human relationships is to recommend and do business with the people with whom we already know, like, and trust. Your job is to build up the widest possible network of influential contacts. The more people you know, and who know you in a positive way, the more likely you are to know the right person at the right time, for the right reason, and for the right opportunity. You will have possibility after possibility of expanding and improving every aspect of your life. When you reach the top of your field by gaining the respect and esteem of the people around you, it will be because you had a goal and a plan, not because of luck.

KEYS FOR BUILDING YOUR NETWORK

1. You attract into your life the people and circumstances that are in harmony with your dominant thoughts.

2. To have more friends, concentrate on being a good friend to others.

3. Make a specific plan for the relationships you want to develop.

4. Self-actualizing individuals are objective and frank about their strengths and weaknesses.

5. Get around the right people. Get around winners, and get away from negative people.

6. Your associations will have more of an impact on your success than any other single choice you make.

Financial Independence

One popular definition of success is being able to live your life your own way. Money is closely associated with freedom, happiness, opportunity, and full self-expression. And there is no area where the concept of luck is more prevalent than in financial success.

The good news is that we are living in the best time in history. We have entered into the Golden Age. As a result of exploding information and knowledge, expanding technology, and increasing competition, there are more opportunities today for the creative minority to achieve financial independence than have ever existed before. And the United States is the best country, offering the greatest number of opportunities of any nation in the world.

There Is Plenty for Everyone

The law of abundance says that we live in a universe of unlimited abundance, and there is plenty for everyone. It used to be that you needed land, labor, capital, furniture, fixtures, buildings, equipment, and other capital resources to create goods and services that you could sell, make a profit on, and accumulate wealth. Today all you need is your brainpower, and you have advantages greatly in excess of people whose entire wealth is tied up in factories and equipment that can quickly be rendered obsolete by a change in technology on the other side of the world.

We live in a universe of unlimited abundance,
and there is plenty for everyone.

People continually ask me how they can change their lives or start a new business if they don't have any money. The fact is that there are hundreds, if not thousands, of businesses that you can get into for less than $100, but they require mental and physical capital, rather than financial capital, to build.

The primary equity that you have to put into any new enterprise is sweat equity: your willingness to work very hard to achieve your goals. If you have that, everything else will take care of itself.

Everyone wants to be financially independent. Why should you want to be wealthy? Why should you pay off all your bills and have money in the bank? Why do you want financial abundance in the first place?

Let me give you my answer to those questions. You inevitably attract into your life the thoughts and pictures that you most emotionalize, so if you're worried about money all the time, you will invariably attract more money problems. Fully 80 percent of American families today have no savings. Fully 70 percent of working Americans have no discretionary income. They spend everything they make, every single paycheck—and usually a little bit more, on credit cards—and have nothing left over. Someone once wrote that the average American family is only two paychecks away from homelessness. If their income is cut off for any period of time, they will be in desperate straits.

A person without money is like a person who has not eaten for a long time: he or she is totally preoccupied with that lack. Just as the hungry person thinks about food all the time, to the exclusion of almost everything else, a person with financial problems worries about money all the time and has very little emotional or spiritual energy left over to spend on the world around them.

Money is what the psychologist Frederick Herzberg called a *hygiene factor*. He said you need a certain amount to assure a reasonable level of financial and physical security. Below that point, you think of nothing else. Above that point, you begin to think of other things that are important to you.

Wealthy people will tell you that money is only a scorecard. Once you've achieved a certain level of financial success, you're no longer preoccupied with money, so you turn your attention to other things: your health, your relationships, and the contribution you can make to the world around you. You become more interested in other people. You become more oriented toward inner development and personal growth. You appreciate literature, philosophy, and music. You get more pleasure out of doing things with the important people in your life.

At a certain level, money is no longer your main preoccupation, and your whole life improves, but below a certain point, you think of nothing else. You get up in the morning; you think and worry about money all day long. The number one reason for marital breakdowns in the United States is arguments about money. One of the major sources of stress, anxiety, and personality problems is worries about money, which become all-consuming.

Consequently, you owe it to yourself to achieve financial security and eventually financial independence. Your long-term goal must be to build a financial fortress of assets, properly deployed, so that you never have to worry about money again.

You owe it to yourself to achieve financial independence.

Fortunately, because there are so many rags to riches stories in the United States, we have more ideas and information on achieving financial independence today than we could apply if we lived a hundred lifetimes.

Do What Successful People Do

The law of emulation says you will be successful to the exact degree to which you find out what other successful people do, and you do the same things. This is so obvious that most people miss it completely. I am astonished by the number of people who are trying to succeed in a career or business without studying the other successful people in that area. They are trying to reinvent the wheel.

My late friend Kop Kopmeyer, who studied success for fifty-four years, said that one of the most critical success principles he ever discovered was the need to learn from the experts. You don't have enough time on earth to figure it all out by yourself. If you want to be successful, you must find out who is already enjoying the kind of success you desire, learn what they did and are doing now, and do the same things yourself until you get the same results.

Of course, you probably recognize this as a restatement of the law of cause and effect. Instead of wasting years trying to blaze a brand-new trail, read the books, listen to the audio programs, and attend the courses of other people who have started from nothing and accomplished wonderful things with their lives. Do exactly what they did until you master their skills and abilities before going off on your own with your own ideas.

To become a master chef takes about seven years. The finest cooking school in the world is the Swiss Culinary Institute in Geneva. A person starts at the Swiss Culinary Institute peeling fruits and vegetables. They do this for the entire first year until they develop a tremendous sense for the texture and feel of fruits and vegetables in all states of freshness, flavor, and composition. In the second year, they move on to salads and other preparations of fruits and vegetables. In each subsequent year, they spend hundreds of hours working with individual spices, sauces, ingredients, meats, and combinations.

At the end of seven years, the student graduates as one of the finest chefs in the world. They then go to work in an internship under a master chef in a top restaurant. In another three to five years, the chef will be ready to strike out on their own. The finest hotels and restaurants in the world are those that have been able to hire graduates of the Swiss school. These people are paid extraordinary amounts of money and retire financially independent.

Before these individuals became creative, innovative chefs, they mastered every stage of cooking as it had been learned and passed on over the years by the finest chefs in the world. They did not begin to improve or innovate before they were thoroughly educated at a high level of basic skills.

The law of value says that all wealth comes about as a result of increasing value. The primary sources of value today are time and knowledge. Your ability to acquire the key knowledge, ideas, insights, and skills that you need and apply them to improve the life or work of someone else determines the financial rewards that you will enjoy. There is no other way to permanently enjoy those rewards.

To state the law of value another way, you must constantly focus on increasing your contribution to the world. Customer benefit, customer value, and improving the lives of others are the true source of lasting value and ultimate wealth.

Seven Secrets of Value

There are seven secrets for increasing value. Any one of them can be sufficient for you to become financially successful. When you begin to combine these ideas, you will move ahead more rapidly in your financial life than you ever have before.

SPEED

Increase the speed with which you deliver value. Everybody's impatient. A person who didn't realize that he wanted your product or service until today now wants it yesterday. People perceive a direct correlation between speed and value. A person who can do it for you fast is considered to be a better and more competent person, offering a higher level of quality than one who does it slowly or whenever he or she gets around to it. Every single innovation in business today is about decreasing the amount of time and increasing the speed that it takes to satisfy customers. Every technological advance is aimed at reducing the amount of time required by a given process.

People perceive a direct correlation
between speed and value.

Management buzzwords, such as reengineering, restructuring, reorganization, and reinventing, have to do with streamlining the process of creating and delivering goods and services so that companies can get them to their customers faster than their competitors. All you need is one good idea that is 10 percent new, better, or different than the way things are being done today, and you may have the starting point of a great fortune. Smartphones enable people to make and take phone calls instantly wherever they are. Federal Express has built a $45 billion industry on delivering letters and packages by the next morning. Speed is at the center of many of the most rapidly growing businesses and personal fortunes.

Look at your industry and your job. Where do you see opportunities to deliver value to your customers faster than it has been done today? How could you shave a second, a minute, an hour, or a day off of delivery times? General Motors used to take four years to design a new automobile. Then the Japanese streamlined their development system so that they could come up with a new car in eighteen months. Now all the major car companies are working to reduce the design, development, and distribution time to below one year. And each new speed record in satisfying customers becomes the minimum that the next competitor has to match. Keep thinking, every day, about how you could speed up the process of delivering your products and services to your customers. It's a real source of value.

QUALITY

The second key to creating wealth is by offering better quality than your competitors at the same price. Quality is whatever the customer says it is. Total quality management can best be defined as finding out what your customers really wants and giving it to them faster than your competitors. Quality does not just mean greater durability or excellence in design. It refers, first of all, to utility, to the use that the customer intends to put the product or service. It is the specific need or benefit that the customer seeks that defines quality in his or her mind.

Extensive interviews with customers make it clear that to them, quality includes not only the product or service, but the way it is delivered. This is why McDonald's could be said to offer excellent quality in terms of the customer's desire for speed, value, cleanliness, and price. McDonald's does not try to compete with gourmet restaurants, but gives the mass of customers exactly what they want in the form and at the price they want it.

How can you increase the quality of what you do in terms of what your customer really wants? Here's a key: listen for complaints. In fact, you should regularly ask your customers if they have any suggestions for improving your products or services. If you honestly invite feedback from your customers, they will give you insights into what you can do to satisfy them even more. These insights can give you the winning edge in your marketplace.

Sometimes people equate speed with quality. Domino's Pizza has built a billion-dollar industry by delivering pizzas within thirty minutes. To the hungry purchaser of a pizza, speed is quality and quality is speed.

ADD VALUE

The third key to wealth is by looking for ways to add value to everything you do. Remember, everyone in a given industry is offering the same thing. These factors become the basic minimum, or the expected norm, in the market. If you want to stand out, you have to *plus* whatever you're doing so that your customer perceives you and your offering as being superior to that of your competitors.

You can add value to a product or service by improving the packaging or design, and by simplifying its method of use. Apple transformed the world of computers by making them easy to use for the unsophisticated person. Simplicity became an enormous source of added value for Apple and countless other companies that have followed the same route.

A salesperson adds value by asking better questions, listening more attentively, and carefully tailoring and customizing their product or service to exactly what the customer wants. As a result, the customer perceives that the salesperson is a more valuable resource than another salesperson who doesn't pay such close attention.

CONVENIENCE

The fourth key to increasing wealth is by increasing the convenience of purchasing and using your product or service. Fast-food stores are a simple example of how much more people are willing to pay for convenience. They pay 15 to 20 percent more per product if they don't have to drive to a grocery store.

Cash machines, which are open twenty-four hours per day, offer an example of how banks have been able to increase their perceived value by making it easier for customers to make deposits and withdrawals. Drive-in windows at fast-food operations are another example. Speedy pickup and delivery of any product or service makes it easier for the customer to patronize you

How could you increase the ease with which customers use your product or services? How could you make it so easy to deal with you that your customers could not even conceive of dealing with anyone else?

How could you make it so easy to deal
with you that your customers could not
even conceive of dealing with anyone else?

CUSTOMER SERVICE

The fifth key to creating value is improving customer service. People are predominantly emotional: they are greatly affected by the friendliness, cheerfulness, and helpfulness of customer service representatives. Many companies are using customer service as a primary source of competitive advantage in a fast-changing marketplace. Nordstrom is one of the most successful department store chains in America, not because they have different products, but because they give the warmest and friendliest customer service of any major retail operation in the country.

Walmart has gone from being an obscure department store in Bentonville, Arkansas, to being the biggest retailer in the world by being a fast, friendly, happy place to shop. When Walmart employees get older, they are turned into greeters. They stand at the doors of stores and welcome the customers coming in, thanking them for shopping at Walmart. As a result of these innovations, Walmart founder Sam Walton created a fortune starting back in the 1940s with nothing but a bankrupt store and an old pickup truck. In late 2022, Walmart's net worth was $429 billion.

Where do you see ways to improve customer service so you can gain a winning edge over your competitors? The ways that you can do your job better and satisfy your customers more are virtually unlimited, except by your own imagination.

CHANGING LIFESTYLES

The sixth key to creating wealth is changing lifestyles, and the impact they're having on customer purchasing patterns and behaviors throughout the country.

More and more people are becoming senior citizens. There's also a national trend toward cocooning, or staying at home more and making the home environment more enjoyable. Young people's tastes are very different from those of young people a generation ago. More people want to travel and take vacations, thereby creating a boom in the travel and leisure industries. Changing lifestyles and demographics can create opportunities that will enable you to offer a product or service to a clearly identifiable market that can make you wealthy in a short period of time.

What trends do you see that you can exploit by offering new and better products and services? How can you reorganize and redesign your efforts to appeal to customers with new, better, different, and cheaper products and services?

DISCOUNTING

The seventh key to creating wealth is just plain discounting: selling higher volumes of products and services to more and more people at lower and lower prices. You've heard it said that if you want to dine with the classes, you have to sell to the masses. You see incredible success stories like Costco, offering warehouses full of bulk, low-priced products, with people coming from miles around and jamming the parking lots from dawn until dusk.

How could you offer a product or service of good value at a lower price? How could you squeeze out the costs of getting the product to customers, passing the savings on to them?

When you think of increasing the speed of delivering your product or service, improving quality, adding value, increasing convenience, giving better customer service, catering to changing lifestyles and trends, and reducing the cost, you will be astonished at the incredible number of possibilities all around you. One idea for benefiting customers in a way that no one else is doing can launch you into financial success.

How to Become Financially Independent

Tens of thousands of self-made millionaires have been interviewed and studied. The research shows that most of them started with nothing, from blue-collar backgrounds and with limited educations. Many never finished high school. Many continue to live in the same neighborhood, and only they know that they are worth more than $1 million. People living on either side of them may be earning more money on a month-to-month basis but may also have continuing financial crises in their lives. Self-made millionaires are very different in their approach toward time, money, and life.

Here's a simple process you can follow to become financially independent. It's guaranteed to work. It works for every single person who tries it. It's a way of implementing some of the laws of luck in your life and making these factors work for you.

To become financially independent, the first thing you must do is to set it as a goal. Get serious; stop fooling around. Everybody wishes, hopes, and prays that someday something wonderful will happen to save them from their financial problems, but you know the truth. You know you are responsible, and if anything that's going to happen for you or to you, it is going to happen because of you.

If you want to be worth a certain amount of money over the course of the next ten or twenty years, write it down as a goal, make a plan, and set a timeline back to the current day. Set subgoals and subdeadlines on those goals from now into the months and the years ahead. Make a plan of how you're going to achieve that goal and what you're going to do at every step of the way. The more detailed your plan for earning money and investing it, the more likely it is to come true for you.

Once you have a clear goal and a plan for financial attainment, you must ask yourself the key question: what must you excel at doing in order to earn the money that you will need to earn to achieve these goals? You then set a new set of goals to develop these skills and become very good at what you do. You commit to investing any amount of time, money, and effort in becoming the kind of person you need to become to deserve the money that you wish to acquire.

My late friend, motivational speaker Jim Rohn, used to point out that the most important part of becoming a millionaire is being the kind of person you have to be inside in order to be a millionaire on the outside. Once you have become that kind of person, even if you lose the money, you will make it all back again, because you will have created the mental equivalent required for financial success. You will attract new opportunities and possibilities if you have become a millionaire in your own thinking.

Becoming a millionaire requires moving from positive thinking to positive knowing. You must move from wishing and hoping to absolutely knowing that you are the kind of person with the skills and attitude that it takes to achieve financial success. Once you have that attitude, no one can take it away from you. Throughout your life, you must keep a long-term vision of your financial goals in front of you, along with a short-term focus on doing the things that you have to do extremely well in order to deserve the money you want to earn.

Becoming a millionaire requires moving
from positive thinking to positive knowing.

The Law of Saving

The law of saving is the key factor that ensures that you will achieve your goals of financial independence. This law says that if you save and invest 10 percent of your income over the course of your working lifetime, you will retire a millionaire. In the third quarter of 2022, median weekly earnings of full-time workers were $1,070, which on an annual basis is $55,640. If you were to save 10 percent of that and you were to carefully invest it at an average of 10 percent interest over the course of your working lifetime, it would be worth more than $1 million; you would retire rich. There are many investment plans whereby you can save money and defer taxes. These amounts grow with the power of compound interest and over a working lifetime will enable you to achieve all your financial goals.

Now you may be thinking that because you have so many bills and expenses, you could never even think of saving 10 percent of your income. But as the late businessman and philanthropist W. Clement Stone said, if you cannot save money, the seeds of greatness are not in you.

"If you cannot save money, the seeds
of greatness are not in you."
—W. Clement Stone

If you can't save 10 percent of your income, you can at least save 1 percent. Get yourself a piggy bank or a jar and put it on your dresser. Each night when you come home, put the equivalent of 1/30 of 1 percent of your monthly income into the jar. Say you earn $4,000 a month. Since 1 percent of $4,000 is $40 per month, 1/30 of $40 is $1.33 per day. Anyone can save $1.33 per day. Instead of having that extra cup of coffee, soda, or cigarette, put the money into the jar. At the end of the month, take the $40 down to the bank and put it into a special savings account. I call this a special savings account because it is not a place where you save for a new car, a refrigerator, or a motor home. This is money that you put away for financial independence. This is money that you resolve to never touch or spend, for any reason. Once you've put it away, as far as you're concerned, it is gone forever.

You learn to live on the other 99 percent of your income until you get comfortable with that. You then increase your savings rate to 2 percent of your income. Soon you will find yourself saving 10 percent of your income off the top and living on the other 90 percent without any problem at all. Moreover, you will find yourself being much more financially responsible in every other area of your life. Both your expenses and your bills will start to come down on a month-by-month basis.

But here's the most wonderful thing. It's a critical luck factor, called the law of accumulation. As you save little bits of money and invest it with your emotions of hope and desire, it develops a force field of energy around it and begins to attract more money to go with it.

You've heard it said that it takes money to make money. This is true. The force of attraction exerted by the money in your bank account will grow, expand, and attract more money and more opportunities to increase your income. The bigger this amount grows, the more money it will attract to you, just as a more powerful magnet attracts pieces of metal from further away. You will start to get small bonuses and unexpected pay increases; you will sell things from your garage and get cash, people will pay back old loans, and you will get income tax refunds that you hadn't expected. In every case, this is the law of accumulation and the law of attraction at work. You must take these extra bits of money and put them away, building up your financial account until it gets larger and larger.

The law of opportunity, another key luck factor, will then kick in. This law says that when you are ready, exactly the right opportunity will appear to you at exactly the right time. When you've built up your financial storehouse, you will get opportunities to invest that money in places that will grow it even more rapidly. Often you'll get an opportunity for a business or a second income, and you will have the money to take advantage of it.

When you are ready, exactly the right opportunity
will appear to you at exactly the right time.

This opportunity money is one of the greatest joys of life. A person with money in the bank and bills under control is a totally different person psychologically than one with an empty bank account who's worried about bills at the end of every month. By having money, you become a more positive and optimistic person, you create a force field of energy, and you attract into your life more people, ideas, opportunities, and resources to help you to move more rapidly towards your goal.

Two Major Dangers

There are two major dangers that can sabotage your desires to be financially independent. The first is Parkinson's law, which says that expenses always rise to meet income. In order to succeed, you must consciously, deliberately, and regularly break Parkinson's law. Your expenses may rise as your income increases, but you must never allow them to rise so high that they consume everything you're earning. This can be fatal. If you get a salary increase of 10 percent, save 50 percent or more of it and improve your standard of living with the other 50 percent. But whatever you do, don't get into the habit of spending it all and a little more besides.

The second danger that can sabotage your dreams of financial success is the get-rich-quick mentality. This is the desire to get money easily without working or paying the full price for it in advance. An old Japanese proverb says that making money is like digging in the sand with a pin, while losing money is like pouring water on the sand. The only thing easy about money is losing it.

Once you have begun to put your money away, institute the luck factor called the law of investing. This says that you must investigate before you invest. You must spend at least as much time studying the investments as you spend earning the money. You must thoroughly understand the investment before you part with your hard-earned cash. If it takes you a year to save $2,000 and then lose it in a poorly thought-out investment, you have not just lost the money, you have lost a solid year of hard work. You have been financially set back for an irreplaceable year in your life.

Three Legs of Financial Independence

The final law of money is the law of conservation: it is not how much you earn but how much you keep that counts. It's amazing how many people earn an extraordinary amount of money over the their working lifetimes and end up dependent on relatives and Social Security when their working years are over.

The three legs of the stool of financial independence are *savings*, *investment*, and *insurance*. Save and set aside two to six months of expenses, and put it in a money market account or a balanced mutual fund, where it can be turned into cash in case of an emergency. Then carefully invest in things you have thoroughly studied, or with successful people whom you thoroughly know and trust. Finally, you should properly insure your home, car, life, possessions, and business. Many people ruin their lives by trying to save a couple of dollars on insurance premiums.

Financial accumulation should be based on the ratchet effect: each time you achieve a certain financial level, you should lock it in by carefully managing and monitoring your money and insuring against any untoward event that might occur. All long-term money is serious money, and all serious money is conservative money.

Finally, the best investment you can make is in yourself: getting better and better at the skills that enable you to earn the money in the first place. You can get the equivalent of a university education every year if you read an hour or two a day, listen to audio programs in your car, and attend seminars and courses on a regular basis. This type of education will add 10 to 20 percent, or even more, to your annual income every year. I have met countless people who have doubled and tripled their income in as little as a year by investing in themselves and upgrading their skills.

When you become outstanding at doing what you do, you will be paid very well for it. When you're paid very well and you consciously violate Parkinson's law, you save more and more of your increasing earnings. You will invest that money carefully in things you know about and with people you trust. By the miracle of compound interest, you will get out of debt, build up a financial fortress, and eventually achieve financial independence. People around you will tell you how lucky you have been, but you will know the truth.

KEYS TO FINANCIAL INDEPENDENCE

1. All wealth comes about as a result of increasing value. The primary sources of value today are time and knowledge.
2. There are seven secrets for increasing value: speed; quality; adding value to a product; convenience; customer service; and understanding changing lifestyles.
3. If you save and invest 10 percent of your income over the course of your working lifetime, you will retire a millionaire.
4. As you save and invest your money with hope and desire, it attracts more money to go with it.

5. You must consciously violate Parkinson's law, which says that expenses rise to meet increasing income.

6. The three legs of the stool of financial independence are *savings*, *investment*, and *insurance*.

8

Using the Power
of Your Mind

Your mind is the most incredible asset you could ever have. There is not a problem you cannot solve, an obstacle you cannot overcome, or a goal that you cannot achieve when you tap into the incredible powers of your brain. You are a potential genius; you have the capacity to function at far higher levels of intelligence and creativity than you ever have.

According to current knowledge, your brain has 86 billion cells. Each of these cells is connected and interconnected, like Christmas tree lights, with as many as 20,000 other cells. This means that the possible combinations and permutations of thought available to you is a number greater than that of all the known atoms in the universe.

Your brain has enormous reserve capacities as well. There are medical histories of people who have lost as much as 90 percent of their brains as a result of accidents. They have been able to function effectively with the remaining 10 percent, even getting straight A's in school.

According to the Brain Institute at Stanford University, the average person uses not 10 percent of their potential, as commonly been believed, but closer to 2 percent. The average person functions at very low levels of output and performance. There are more than 1 million words in the English language, but the average person uses only about 1,200 in a given day. About 85 percent of all English conversation takes place using only 2,000 words, and fully 95 percent of conversation is covered by 4,000 words out of over 1,000,000 words available.

Why is word usage so important? It's because each word is a thought. The more words you know and can use, the higher and more complex thoughts you can think. People with limited vocabularies have limited thinking abilities. You can dramatically increase a person's intelligence merely by increasing his or her vocabulary over time. Each word you learn makes you aware of as many as another ten words. As a result, if you were to learn one new word per day, 365 days per year, in a year or two you would be one of the smartest people in our society.

The more words you know, the higher and more complex thoughts you can think.

People who are considered lucky have learned how to activate and use more of their brainpower than the average person. They have learned to tune into their intelligence at will. When you activate your incredible mind, you will accomplish things that will amaze everyone around you.

Concentration and Decision

The law of concentration says that whatever you dwell upon grows and increases in your life. Applied to brain power, this law says the more you concentrate on any thought, problem, or goal, the more of your mental capacity is activated and focused on solving that problem.

The law of decision is also a major luck factor. It says that any clear, specific decision to do something definite clears your mind and activates your creativity. When you're indecisive, when you can't make up your mind whether or not to do a certain thing, you seem to go back and forth, and you become easily distracted. Sometimes you get tired and depressed. But when you firmly decide upon a goal or action, suddenly you feel bright and optimistic again, you feel positive and refreshed. You have a surge of energy, and you feel back in control of your life once more. Again, your conscious mind commands, and your subconscious mind obeys. Your subconscious mind goes to work to bring your goals into reality.

The Ultimate Faculty

But the most powerful faculty you have is your superconscious mind. It is the source of all inspiration, imagination, intuition, insights, ideas, and even hunches. It is the powerhouse that, when activated properly, can bring you everything you want.

The existence of this superconscious mind has been known throughout the centuries. Ralph Waldo Emerson called it the Oversoul. Napoleon Hill referred to it as Infinite Intelligence. He discovered that every wealthy man in America had gotten there by learning how to tap into his superconscious mind on a regular basis. The superconscious mind has been called the universal subconscious mind, the superconscious, and the collective unconscious. Every technological breakthrough, every work of art, every exquisite piece of music or literature, every flash of genius demonstrates the power of the superconscious mind.

The law of superconscious activity is the most important of all luck factors. It says that any thought, plan, goal, or idea that you hold continuously in your conscious mind must be brought into reality by your superconscious mind. Just imagine: you can have anything you really want if you can think about it, dwell upon it, emotionalize it, visualize it, and affirm it over and over again. The true test of how intensely you want something is your capacity to think about it all the time.

Your superconscious mind has seven key capabilities, plus many more that we can't go into here. You will recognize the times that your superconscious mind has worked in the past when you compare these capabilities against your previous experiences.

GOAL-ORIENTED MOTIVATION

Your superconscious mind is capable of goal-oriented motivation. When you are positive, excited, and working toward the accomplishment of clear goals that are important to you, you will feel a continuous flow of energy and motivation. In fact, your superconscious mind is a source of free energy. When you are totally involved with accomplishing something that you really care about, you will need less sleep, work longer, harder hours, and feel terrific about yourself throughout. You will seldom be sick or depressed. You are unlikely to have headaches or physical symptoms. You will feel as though you're on a psychological high, and indeed you are. The more you write and rewrite your goals, and the more you both imagine and emotionalize the achievement of those goals, the more motivated you will be and the more energy you will have.

SUBCONSCIOUS ACTIVATION

Your superconscious mind is activated by clear commands and affirmations to your *subconscious.* Whenever you convey a powerful thought from your conscious mind to your subconscious, you activate your superconscious mind as well. Whenever you visualize your goals exactly as you would like to see them in reality, you stimulate your superconscious mind to bring those goals into realization.

There are four principal aspects of visualization for stimulating your superconscious powers: *vividness, duration, intensity,* and *frequency.*

With regard to *vividness,* there is a direct relationship between how clearly you can see the details of your goal in your mind's eye and how rapidly it appears in your reality. When you begin visualizing, your goals will be fuzzy, indistinct, and indeterminate. But the more you visualize, the more clearly you will see your goals and the more rapidly your goals will move toward you.

Duration of a visualization refers to how long you can hold a mental picture of your goal in your mind. The longer you can hold your mental pictures (especially just before you fall off to sleep or when you're daydreaming), the more rapidly this picture stimulates and activates your superconscious mind.

The *intensity* of your visualization refers to the amount of emotion that you can put behind your mental picture. The more excited and happy you are about the goal you're imagining, the greater impact it has on your superconscious.

The fourth part of visualization is *frequency*, which refers to the number of times every day that you visualize your goal as a reality or see yourself performing exactly the way you wish to perform. One key to learning any skill is visualizing yourself using that skill. One key to becoming excellent in any sport is to relax and see yourself performing perfectly in competition. A key to physical fitness is to visualize yourself as the kind of person you would like to be. An essential part of self-confidence is to repeatedly see yourself performing with calmness and confidence in any important area of your life.

The more you visualize with vividness, duration, intensity, and frequency, the more you program yourself internally so that you will walk, talk, think, and perform on the outside in a manner that is exactly consistent with the mental pictures that you have impressed onto your subconscious and superconscious mind.

SOLVING—AND CREATING—PROBLEMS

The third quality of your superconscious mind is that it automatically solves every problem on the way to your goal—as long as your goal is clear. In addition, your superconscious mind will actually give you the learning experiences that you need to achieve that goal that you have set for yourself.

Often when you set a new goal, your life will go off in a totally unexpected direction. Many people have set goals to increase their incomes over the coming years and then found themselves fired or laid off. Later, they got a new job or started a business, and in retrospect they saw that they would never have achieved their financial goals if they had continued in the old position.

Often when you set a new goal, your life will
go off in a totally unexpected direction.

Most successful men and women in America will admit that their great success came as a result of the unexpected loss of a job or collapse of an enterprise. As a result, they made different decisions and implemented changes that put them onto a new track. There they achieved the goals that they would never have attained if they hadn't lost that previous job.

Most people achieve their great successes in an industry different from where they originally started. As long as they were absolutely clear about their ultimate goal of financial independence, their superconscious minds guided them from experience to experience, solving every problem as they moved unerringly toward eventual accomplishment.

THE RIGHT ANSWER AT THE RIGHT TIME

The fourth quality of your superconscious mind is that it brings you exactly the answer you need at exactly the right time. For example, you may be thinking about your goal and suddenly get an inspiration to phone somebody that you haven't talked to for a long time. When you call that person, it may turn out that he or she has a priceless piece of information which is exactly what you need to take the next step. If you can visualize the other person clearly enough, in many cases they will phone. How many times has it happened that you have thought of another person, and within a couple of minutes the phone has rung, with that person on the line? This is an example of the superconscious mind in action.

CONCENTRATION AND DISTRACTION

The fifth quality of your superconscious mind is that it operates best under two conditions. You must use both of these conditions continually on every problem or on every goal. The first condition is when you're concentrating single-mindedly, with your total attention, on solving a problem or achieving a goal. The second condition is when your mind is completely busy elsewhere. Below, I will give you some techniques to activate your superconscious mind using both of these approaches.

PREPROGRAMMING

Number six, your superconscious mind is capable of preprogramming. You can give a command from your conscious mind through your subconscious to your superconscious, which will act upon the command at exactly the right time, in exactly the right way.

For example, you can preprogram your mind to wake up at any time you want, anywhere, no matter how many time zones you may have changed. You never need to use an alarm clock again. If you want to wake up at 6:30 a.m., you can program the idea into your mind and simply go to sleep. At 6:30 a.m., even if it's completely dark in the room, you will snap out of sleep and be wide awake.

You can use your superconscious mind to find parking places in crowded areas. I know people who never have any problems finding a parking space wherever they go. You do this simply by relaxing and visualizing a space opening up when you arrive at your destination. In almost every case, if you have prepared your mind and your goal is clear, the parking space will either be there or open up as you arrive.

You can also preprogram your superconscious mind with a question or problem before you fall asleep. Clearly articulate the problem as a question, and turn it over to your superconscious mind as you drift off. The next morning, you will open your eyes, and while you're getting up and getting going, the exact answer for you, in the exact form that you need it, will appear. Sometimes it will be a sudden flash of intuition; another time it will be a comment from your spouse or an early phone call. Often it will be something that appears in your morning newspaper.

In any case, you should use this preprogramming faculty continually. Every night before you go to bed, program every problem you have into your superconscious mind and ask for a solution. Then just forget about it until the solution appears.

CONSISTENCY WITH SELF-CONCEPT

The seventh quality, and perhaps the most important function, of your superconscious mind is that it makes all your words and actions and their effects fit a pattern consistent with your self-concept and your dominant goals. Your superconscious mind will guide you to say and do exactly the right things at exactly the right time for you. Your superconscious mind will also stop you from saying or doing things that would turn out to be inappropriate or incorrect. It functions best in a mental climate of calm, confident, positive expectation. The more completely relaxed, trusting, and accepting you are that everything is working together for your benefit, the more rapidly your superconscious mind works to bring you what you want.

Your superconscious mind functions best in a mental climate of calm, confident, positive expectation.

As you've probably figured out by now, your superconscious mind is the true seat of the power of attraction. As you continually affirm, visualize, and emotionalize your goals with an attitude of calm, confident expectation, you stimulate the power of attraction and draw into your life the people and circumstances that you need, exactly as and when you need them, to enable you to achieve the goals that are most important to you. When you systematically unleash the power of your superconscious mind, you will achieve more in a couple of years than most people do in a lifetime.

Common Sense

A key luck factor is good judgment, or what is often called common sense. Common sense is often defined as an ability to recognize patterns that you have seen in the past. Continually evaluating your experiences can give you invaluable ideas and insights for success. As you acquire more and more knowledge and experience, you will be able to come to faster and better conclusions with less and less information. You will see the outlines of a pattern and move quickly to a conclusion because of your past experience and your ability to recognize the key factors. As they say, you will be able to connect the dots faster.

Your superconscious mind serves an invaluable role in improving your judgment and increasing your common sense. It enables you to see a situation in its entirety and know intuitively what to do and say the next moment. Men and women become great when they listen to their inner voices and trust their intuitions. You achieve extraordinary things when you combine your conscious knowledge, your subconscious memory of previous experiences, and your superconscious capacity to incorporate your previous knowledge and skill into new ideas and insights.

Mindstorming

There are two ways to stimulate your superconscious mind. One is passive, and the other is active. You should use both on every problem.

Let's start off with the active methods. Perhaps the most powerful one is mindstorming. More people have become successful using this simple technique than by the use of any other ever discovered. Once you begin using it, your life will take off as though you have just jammed your foot down on your own accelerator. I've taught this mindstorming technique for years, and everyone who has ever tried it has been astonished at the immediate improvements that begin to take place in their lives.

The mindstorming method is straightforward: Take a piece of paper, and at the top, write down your goal or problem in the form of a question. Make it as specific and as clear as possible so that your mind can become actively engaged in developing answers. For example, if you want to increase your income by 25 percent over the next twelve months, and you are currently earning $100,000 per year, you could write a question such as, "How can I increase my income by 25 percent over the next twelve months?" An even better way of writing the question would be, "What can I do to earn $125,000 over the next twelve months?" Your choice of a question will have a major impact on the quality of the answers that emerge.

Once you've written down the question, write twenty answers to it. This is very important: you must generate a minimum of twenty answers to your question, and it's not as easy as it seems. Of course, the first three to five will be easy. You will come up with simple ideas like "work harder," "work longer," or "take additional training." The next five to ten answers will be far more difficult, and the last ten to twenty will be the most difficult, but this exercise is most effective when you concentrate on finding more and more answers to the same question.

Countless students in my seminars have found that their twentieth answer is exactly the insight they were looking for. One businessman who had been struggling with a problem for six months came up with the perfect solution with the twentieth answer the very first time he tried this process.

Once you've generated twenty answers, review them, and select at least one that you will act on immediately. This too is very important: the faster you act on a new idea, the greater will be the subsequent flow of new ideas focused on that goal or problem. The more ideas you try, the more likely you are to do exactly the right thing at exactly the right time, and you will have what other people call luck.

If you were to use this idea five days per week on your major goals or problems, you would generate twenty ideas per day, or 100 ideas per week. Over the course of a year, you would generate 5,000 new ideas (and that's assuming that you don't bother to think on your vacation). If you were to implement one new idea per day, five days per week, fifty weeks per year, you would be implementing 250 new ideas every year. Since the average person only comes up with three or four new ideas each year and usually does nothing with them, your life would sparkle with opportunities and possibilities that you may have never imagined.

Ideas are the keys to the future. Ideas are the ways to achieve goals. Ideas are the ways to overcome obstacles. Ideas are the tools that you use to solve problems. Ideas will make you richer, happier, more satisfied, more content, and successful. New ideas contain all the key elements of luck.

When you use the mindstorming technique first thing every morning, your mind will sparkle with creative ideas all day long. You will see new possibilities and potentials, and you will have ideas for taking advantage of them at every turn. Other people will be amazed at how quickly you come up with different ways to achieve goals and different solutions to persistent problems. And the more you develop a reputation for being highly creative, the more opportunities you will get to use your new creative skills.

With regard to ideas like mindstorming, there are two types of people. There are those who listen, nod enthusiastically, and go home and do nothing. Then there are those—the talented tenth, the small, creative minority—who listen to this idea and act on it immediately.

It's essential to develop the habit of acting on a good idea when you hear it. There's a direct relationship between success and speed of implementation. If you have a great idea or insight and you don't do anything with it, you should not be surprised if nothing changes for you. It's been estimated that you have at least three or four ideas each year, driving to and from work, any one of which would make you a millionaire. How many times have you come up with an idea for a new product or service and done nothing with it? Then, a couple of years later, you've seen someone else make a million dollars with the same idea. The only difference between you and the other person is that you failed to act on your idea, and the other individual took it and ran with it immediately.

Act on a good idea when you hear it.

Don't sell yourself short. The fact that you can come up with an idea or insight to improve the life or work of someone else means that you probably have the capacity to execute that idea. By the law of attraction and the law of superconscious activity, you will attract into your life everything you need to make your goal or plan a reality as long as it is clear and you really want to achieve it.

Mindstorming stimulates your reticular cortex and increases your sensitivity and awareness to a very high degree. You become incredibly perceptive at noticing little things that can be combined with other ideas and insights to create new answers and solutions to help you move ahead more rapidly.

Your superconscious mind is triggered by three factors overall. These are, first, intensely desired goals; second, pressing problems; and third, well-worded questions. Use all three of these as often as you can to maximize your creative abilities. Intensely desired goals, backed by a burning desire, enthusiasm, and excitement, rev up your superconscious mind and stimulate you to higher levels of alertness to the possibilities around you. Pressing problems that you intensely desire to solve, accompanied by regular mindstorming exercises, are wonderful stimulants to creativity. Finally, well-worded questions, perhaps the most dependable way to stimulate new ideas, are often the keys to enhancing your creativity.

Systematic Problem-Solving

Another active method for stimulating your superconscious mind is *systematic problem-solving*. Over the years, I've developed a seven-step method that enables you to use far more of your thinking abilities than you could if you simply threw yourself at an obstacle or difficulty the way most people do.

Systematic problem-solving is a hallmark of genius in every field. Research proves that geniuses approach every difficulty with a specific methodology and process. When you use a systematic method, you begin to function at genius levels as well. In addition, a method enables you to use all of your mental abilities and activates your superconscious mind to give you the insights and ideas you need.

1. Approach the problem with a calm, confident expectation that there is a logical, workable solution waiting to be found. This approach calms you down, relaxes you, and opens your creative mind to be sensitive to all the different ways that you can go about solving this problem. You should assume from the beginning that every problem contains within it the seeds of its own solution. The solution, in effect, is the flip side of the problem. It is just lying there, waiting for you to find it. As I mentioned earlier, your goal is to be solution-oriented rather than problem-oriented and future-oriented rather than past-oriented. When you think and talk in terms of possible solutions, your mind will be calm, positive, bright, clear, and fully functioning.

2. Define the problem as a challenge or as an opportunity. Words are important. They have the power to create emotions, either positive or negative. The choice of certain words in describing a problem can raise or lower blood pressure, heart rate, and respiratory rate. In fact, *problem* itself is often a negative and scary word that causes you to tense up and become worried. Imagine how you feel when somebody calls up and says, "We

have a real problem here." You immediately become uneasy and upset. But if you refer to every problem or difficulty as a challenge or an opportunity, you will begin to look forward to them.

Sometimes I tell my seminar audiences that I know what every one of them does for a living. I can see the faces of disbelief smiling back at me, but the answer is simple: whatever your job title is, your real job is as a problem-solver. Where there are no problems to be solved, there are no jobs. The more difficult, complicated, and expensive the problems, the greater the opportunities there are for you to rise rapidly and earn a wonderful living. The highest-paid people in every industry are the best problem solvers in that industry.

Remember, a goal unachieved is just a problem unsolved. Your job is to find ways up, over, around, and through any obstacle or difficulty in your path. Your ability to do this will determine your quality of life, both at home and at work. Napoleon Hill's wonderful discovery—that "every adversity, every failure, every heartbreak carries the seed of an equal or greater benefit"—is one of the great insights into success. Your job is to see every difficulty as a challenge that has been sent to make you smarter and better. Then look into the difficulty for the advantage or benefit that it might contain.

"Every adversity, every failure, every heartbreak,
carries the seed of an equal or greater benefit."
—*Napoleon Hill*

---

3. Problem or challenge definition. Ask yourself, what exactly is the challenge? Write it down. Define it clearly on paper. A

problem defined is half solved; correct diagnosis is half the cure. Once you have the situation clearly defined, ask yourself, what else is the problem? Well-worded questions are powerful stimulants to creativity. The more different ways you can state and restate your problem, the more different ideas and approaches you will come up with.

If your sales are down, you could define your problem by simply saying that sales are down. But what if you decided to restate the problem in a variety of different ways? You could say something like, "Our sales are not as high as we would like them to be," or, "We are not selling as much of our products or services as we would like." You could even say, "Our competitors are selling more products and services than we are," or, "Our salespeople are not closing enough sales for us to achieve our volume goals, or, "Our customers are buying more products or services from our competitors than they are from us." The more you restate the problem in the form of different questions, the more amenable it becomes to different solutions.

4. Identify all the possible causes of the problem. Look for both the obvious and the hidden causes. Test your assumptions. Ask yourself, "What if we were completely wrong in our approach to this current situation?" If you were doing exactly the opposite thing, what changes would be indicated? Errant assumptions lie at the root of every failure. You may have unconsciously assumed something that is not true about your product, your service, the market, the competition, or your customers. All good scientific research is based on the exhaustive testing of hypotheses or assumptions. What are yours?

5. Define all the possible solutions. Write down all of the obvious solutions, and then some of the not so obvious ones. Pick

solutions that are the opposite of the obvious solutions. Sometimes the solution is to do nothing at all. Sometimes it is to do something totally different. The more solutions you can come up with based on your definition of the problem and the reasons for the problem, the more likely you are to come up with the ideal solution.

6. Make a decision among the solutions. Any decision is usually better than none. A clear, unequivocal decision stimulates creativity, generates energy, and activates your superconscious mind.

Any decision is usually better than none.

---

7. Assign responsibility for implementing the solution and take action and get going as quickly as you can. Many people have changed their lives by going through this process and then capping it off by taking some immediate, specific action. Successful people are not those who make the right decisions all the time; they are those who make their decisions right. As soon as you move toward a solution or implementing a decision, you begin to get feedback from your environment. The feedback enables you to continually self-correct. As you learn and correct your course, you become sharper and better and move faster and faster toward your goal, but nothing happens until you act.

These two active methods, mindstorming and the systematic approach to problem-solving, will enable you to achieve more than you may have imagined possible. But you can engage in another series of activities: passive approaches.

The Passive Approach

The law of relaxation says that in all mental working, effort defeats itself. The more you relax, let go, and turn problems over to your superconscious mind, the more rapidly it goes to work for you.

You can use passive methods to activate your subconscious mind in several ways. Daydreaming is a wonderful way to loosen up your mind and allow flashes of insight to dart into your consciousness. Listening to classical music, going for walks in nature or just sitting relaxed, meditating or contemplating, opens up your mind to inspirations that can save you thousands of dollars and years of hard work.

Perhaps the best method for creative thinking is solitude. You sit completely still for thirty or sixty minutes, not moving, not drinking coffee, not smoking, not even listening to music. Just sit perfectly still and wait in the silence for the voice of inspiration to come to you. You are absolutely clear about what you want, you have used your conscious mind to analyze your problems in detail, and you have used mindstorming to fill your mind with ideas. Then just sit quietly in solitude and wait for the answer. You will receive insights that can change the entire course of your life.

KEYS TO INCREASING BRAINPOWER

1. To improve your power of thinking, increase your vocabulary.
2. The more you concentrate on any problem, the more you activate your mental capacity to solve it.
3. There are four key aspects of visualization: *vividness, duration, intensity,* and *frequency*.

4. Your superconscious mind makes all your words and actions fit a pattern consistent with your self-concept and your dominant goals.

5. You can become great if you listen to your inner voices and trust your intuitions.

6. Use the mindstorming process to solve problems and attain goals.

7. Also use passive methods of problem-solving: daydreaming and meditative solitude.

9

Focus on Results

The ultimate luck factor is your ability to get results for which people are willing to pay you, promote you, advance you, open doors for you, and move you up into the top levels of your profession.

The law of results is in many cases the most important part of luck. It says that your rewards will always be equal to the quality, quantity, and timeliness of the results that you accomplish for other people. Everyone is selfish; everyone is continually tuned into their favorite radio station, WII-FM: "What's in it for me?" We evaluate other people in terms of their ability to help us get the things we want. The people who are most capable of helping us to get us what we want faster and easier are the ones who we reward the most and the soonest.

The law of contribution flows directly from the law of results. It says that your financial rewards in life will always be in direct proportion to the value of the contribution that you make, as that value is determined by other people.

In a market economy, the customer determines all prices, including wages, salaries, and commissions, by the things that they're willing to buy and the quantity in which they're willing to purchase them. Companies do not set wages or salaries, except indirectly; they merely pass on the judgments of the marketplace. They organize the efforts of others and combine them to produce products and services for which people are willing to pay in sufficient quantity to generate a profit that enables the company to continue to survive and grow. You can always increase the quality and quantity of your financial rewards by increasing the quality and quantity of the contribution that you make to others. And, in the long term, there is no other way for you to do it.

Many people are suffering job insecurity and declining income today because the world has changed dramatically in recent decades. Today the most valuable single component of any product or service is the amount of knowledge and skill that goes into it. If a person has not committed himself or herself to continually learning, growing, and developing their skills to a high level, their ability to contribute will decline over time, like the water level in a leaky bucket. They will become worth less and less, and they will eventually suffer layoffs, downsizing, unemployment, and insecurity.

The way to enjoy job security and high rewards is by improving and increasing the results that you can get for others and the contribution that you can make to their lives. By the law of correspondence, your living standards will be a mirror image reflection of your ability to contribute this value.

One of the fastest ways to create more opportunities and come to the attention of the important people in your world is to become an intensely results-oriented person. In study after study, result orientation is a key quality of the highest-paid and most respected people in every field and every society. Good work habits go hand in hand with what people call luck. A person who works efficiently and gets a lot of high-value work done on or before schedule seems to get lucky breaks to do more, higher-valued work.

Good work habits go hand in hand
with what people call luck.

Your Most Valuable Asset

According to Harvard University, a company's most valuable asset is its reputation: how it is known to its customers. A company's reputation is contained in the way people in the marketplace talk about and describe that company. An excellent reputation adds premiums to the prices of the company's products or services. Sony Corporation, for example, has one of the finest reputations in the world for technological innovation. The Sony name on a product can increase the cost and perceived value of that product by 20 or 30 percent, even though it is essentially identical to another product on the same shelf carrying a lesser-known name, with a lesser reputation.

By the same virtue, your most valuable asset is your reputation, especially the way you are perceived by your customers and coworkers. Everything you do to improve the quality of your reputation improves the perceived value of your contribution. If a person is known as someone who does an outstanding job, customers line up to purchase that person's services.

If you went to the doctor and the doctor told you that you have to have a serious operation, what would be your first question?

It would probably be, "Who is the very best doctor to perform this kind of surgery?" Many salespeople and executives think customers are totally preoccupied with price. But price is always relative. If you need a serious operation, you'll never ask, "Who is the cheapest doctor I can get for this operation?" Price is not even a factor if the quality of the product or service were important enough.

When you develop a reputation for being one of the best people in your field, you will be paid far more than the average person, and you will find yourself continually in demand. You will quickly learn that what people want more than anything else is quality of results rather than merely low price.

Who Works Hardest?

In every single organization today, everyone knows who works the hardest, the second hardest, the third hardest, and so on. If efficiency experts were to interview everyone in your company and ask them to rate your fellow employees, you would find that virtually everyone knows and agrees on who works the most and the least, and everyone in between.

People who rise to positions of importance are invariably the hardest-working, most dedicated, and most committed people in that field. They are therefore highly sensitive to other people who are like them. Birds of a feather flock together. There is no faster way to attract the attention and support of people who can help you than to develop a reputation as being one of the hardest workers, if not the hardest.

It is not difficult to double and even triple your output. By using a series of proven methods, you can dramatically increase your results. With these techniques, which are practiced by the highest-performing and highest-paid people in every organization, you will get more done more easily and have more free time than you believe possible right now.

The Nature of Time

There are some key principles with regard to time that you must know. First of all, time is inelastic; it cannot be stretched. It is fixed, and it goes by with an absolute, unstoppable regularity. This is a fact of nature to which you must conform, because it cannot be changed. Time is limited. You can't get any more of it. You have twenty-four fresh hours every single day, and the quality of your life will be determined by how you spend them.

You can tell your true values and beliefs—especially how valuable you consider any part of your life to be—by the amount of your time you are willing to invest in them. You start your life with very little money and lots of time. If you're smart, you will end your life with far less time but will have enough money to be financially independent and comfortable.

Throughout your life, you are engaged in a series of trading activities. You trade time for results, rewards, and satisfactions. At any given time, you can look at where you are today and measure how good a trader you have been in the past. A person who is worth a lot of money at the age of thirty or forty is one who has been an excellent trader in financial terms. He has traded his time for learning, acquiring skills, setting goals, organizing his life, and personal and professional development. As a result, he can now trade his time for high rewards in the marketplace. This must be your goal as well.

Another key point: time cannot be saved. It can only be spent. You can only reallocate time away from low-value activities and toward high-value activities. People are successful because they spend more of their time doing things of high value, which move them toward their goals. People fail because they spend too much of their time doing things of low value or no value, which either move them slowly toward their goals, or even worse, away from them. You are always free to choose. At every moment, you can decide to commit your time to high-value activities or to low-value activities. The sum total of your choices will add up to the total quality of your life. It's always up to you.

Time cannot be saved. It can only be spent.

The law of applied effort says that any goal, task, or activity is amenable to the sustained effort of hard work. There is very little that you cannot accomplish if you are willing to work at it long enough and hard enough and persist in the face of all obstacles until you win. Hard work is and always has been the key to success.

However, there is one reservation: today you are a knowledge worker. Knowledge workers have two primary characteristics. First, they are initially more concerned with determining what is to be done rather than how or when it is to be done. Second, unlike factory workers, they are measured on the basis not of activities but of measurable outcomes that people can count, use, and sell in the marketplace.

The most important thing is to identify in advance exactly what is to be done and in what order of importance. You must then have the self-discipline necessary to do the things you should do, when you should do them, whether you feel like it or not. This is the single most important quality you can develop; it is the essence of character and achievement.

The Long View

Success is largely attitudinal: the critical attitude for success and living a so-called lucky life is your attitude toward time. People with a long time perspective are invariably more successful than people with only a short-term outlook. You develop long-time perspective by planning your life ten and twenty years out into the future. You then trace back to the present day and plan your goals, priorities, and activities in terms of where you want to be in X years from now.

Fewer than 3 percent of Americans have a long time perspective, but they end up at the top of most organizations and control most of the money and assets in our country. For example, by saving $200 a month from the age of twenty on and putting it away into solid mutual funds invested in the American stock market, you will be a millionaire when you retire. If it's as simple as that, why doesn't everyone save throughout their working lifetimes and become millionaires? The answer is lack of time perspective.

The key to a long time perspective is contained in the word *sacrifice*. Delayed gratification has always been the key to economic success. The willingness to engage in short-term sacrifices in order to enjoy long-term security and prosperity is the key to luck and achievement. The unwillingness to delay gratification, the inability to restrain yourself from spending everything you make and a little bit more besides, is the surest recipe for failure ever found.

As I've explained earlier, the very act of saving money changes your character. It develops your self-discipline, makes you more controlled and confident, gives you a greater sense of self mastery, and forces you to engage in short-term pain for long-term gain. On the other end, you also need a short time perspective for your activities, which are meant to achieve those more remote goals.

If I were asked to summarize *success* in two words, I would pick *focus* and *concentration*. The ability to focus on your highest priorities and concentrate single-mindedly on them until they are complete will determine your success more than anything else. You can be the most brilliant person in your field, you can be extraordinarily good-looking, well-educated, personable, and surrounded by many opportunities, but if you cannot focus and concentrate, these attributes will do very little good. You will be easily outstripped by an average person who has developed the discipline to focus and concentrate on accomplishing high-priority activities every minute of the working day. The ability to set clear priorities lies at the heart of personal and life management. All failure comes from misplaced and misdirected priorities. All success comes from the ability to select priorities intelligently and stay with them until the most vital tasks are accomplished.

If I were asked to summarize *success* in two words,
I would pick *focus* and *concentration*.

The power of the sun is warm and gentle until it is concentrated through a magnifying glass on a single spot; then it can burn intensely and cause great fires. A small light bulb may yield a little bit of light, perhaps not even enough to read by, but when that light is concentrated through a laser beam, it can cut through steel. It's the same with focusing and concentrating on priorities consistently and persistently until concentration becomes as natural to you as breathing.

Managing Your Life through Lists

There are several steps to setting clear priorities and getting much more done. The first is making lists of activities and tasks before you begin. The very act of working from a list will increase your productivity by 25 percent the first time you try it. All top time managers and highly productive people use lists. Just as you would not think of going to the grocery store without a list of what they wanted to pick up, you should never embark on your day without a clear list or road map of the activities you wish to accomplish.

There are several kinds of lists. A master list, which should lie at the core of your time management program, includes everything that you can think of that you want to do in the foreseeable future. As something comes up, you jot it down on your master list so that you won't forget it. This list can have hundreds of items, some of which are for two, three, and five years out.

Your second list is your monthly list, which consists of the key things that you have to do in order to be successful at your work, plus items from your master list that you want to get done within the next thirty days. Your weekly list is a more refined version of your monthly list, consisting of the things you want to do this week. Your daily list is a complete blueprint of your day from morning to night.

Always start your day, week, and month with a list. Make lists for everything. Think on paper. All the most productive people constantly think with a pen in their hand. Plan every day in advance. Organize your plan as though it was the most important day of your life and every minute was precious to you. Don't make the mistake of starting with whatever tasks happens to be the most pleasant or the most convenient. Think before you act, and then act efficiently and well.

The formula for evaluating a company is contained in the letters ROI: *return on investment.* Your personal formula for effectiveness is contained in the letters ROTI: *return on time invested.* Everything you achieve will reflect whether or not you're getting a high return for the amount of your life that you are investing in your activities. Your job is to get the highest return possible on everything you do.

> Your job is to get the highest return
> possible on everything you do.

Once you've written out a list for the day (preferably the night before, so that your subconscious mind can work on some of your tasks while you sleep), set priorities on the list. To decide what you're going to do first, second, and not at all, you need to determine the logical and orderly sequence of events that will get you the highest payoff from your time invested.

A simple time management technique is the use of the 80/20 rule. In this context, this rule says that 80 percent of the value of any list of activities will be contained in 20 percent of the items on that list. Sometimes 90 percent of the value of your entire list of activities can be contained in only 10 percent of the items, or one item.

Never give in to the temptation to clear up small things first. Once you have set an order of priority and identified the 20 percent of items that count for the highest results, you start at the top rather than at the middle or bottom. You don't start with small items, because they tend to multiply on you. If you start with small items, at the end of the day you'll still find yourself working on them, and your big tasks and responsibilities will be waiting for your attention. Remember, the consequences of any action determine the value of that action. Anything that can have high-level consequences for your life or work is a high priority. Something with low-level consequences, or none, is always a low priority.

Continually reading, learning, and upgrading your skills is a high priority. The long-term consequences for your life and career can be extraordinary. They may not be urgent activities, but they're vitally important, and they need to be incorporated into your life on a regular basis. On the other hand, taking a coffee break or going for lunch has no consequences. You could take coffee breaks, go for lunch for forty years, and become outstanding at your choice of coffee and menus, but it would have no impact on your accomplishments. Always think in terms of consequences before you begin. What are the likely consequences of doing or not doing something?

The ABCDE Method

This is where the ABCDE method can be extremely helpful. An A task is something that you *must* do; there are serious consequences for doing it or not doing it. It is important to your life and career. People are depending on you to perform in it. It is a top priority. Mark A next to all the top-priority items on your list that absolutely must be done, done well, and done soon.

A B task is something that *should* be done. There are mild consequences for doing it or not doing it. People may be unhappy or inconvenienced if you do not carry it out, but it is not as important as an A item. Never do a B task when there is an A task left undone.

A C task is something that would be nice to do, like a coffee break or lunch, but there are no consequences positive or negative for your future. Socializing with coworkers, reading the newspaper, and calling home are nice things to do, but they have virtually no consequences beyond the current moment.

A D item on your list is something that you *delegate.* Delegate everything you possibly can of lower-order priorities so that you have more time to do the few things that only you can do. Every time you have someone else type a letter, make a phone call, file a contract, or perform a clerical task, you are delegating. Every time you pick up dinner on the way home rather than cooking it, you are delegating the preparation of the dinner and saving yourself one or two hours in preparation and cleanup.

The smartest and most productive people in our society are those who are expert at delegating everything conceivable so that they can have more time to do the one or two things for which they are the most rewarded.

The E in the ABCDE formula stands for *eliminate.* One of the greatest time savers is to completely eliminate something that you've been doing in the past that is no longer as valuable or important as something else that you have to do in the present. Setting priorities means setting posteriorities as well.

Your schedule is already full. If you're like most people, you have more than 100 percent of your time already spoken for. In order to have time to do new things, you must stop doing old things. Getting in means getting out. Starting up means stopping off. Setting posteriorities—things that you are going to discontinue either partially or altogether—is one of the fastest ways to free up your schedule for your highest-priority tasks.

What are your posteriorities? What tasks have you inherited over the months and years that are no longer as valuable and important to you as other things that you have to do right now? Your ability to answer this question is a key determinant of your effectiveness.

Five Key Questions

There are five key questions for getting greater results and producing more than anyone else around you. You must ask, answer, and act upon these five questions every minute and every hour of every day.

1. What are your highest-value activities? What do you do that contributes the most value to your company, your life, your work, and your rewards? If you're not sure about the answer, give it some thought. Talk it over with your boss and your coworkers; discuss it with your spouse. You must be crystal clear about your highest-value activities: you can't hit a target that you can't see. You cannot move ahead rapidly in your career if you do not know the key tasks that you must do in order to be successful and be promoted.

What are your highest-value activities?

---

2. The second question is similar to the first: what are your key result areas? What specific results or outcomes have you been hired to accomplish? Of all the things you do, what are

the measurable, specific items for which you are completely responsible, and upon which your success and your career depends? You must clearly identify your key result areas and concentrate on doing them in an excellent fashion every day, all day long.

3. Why are you on the payroll? Why do they give you money for what you do? If you were to explain or justify the money you receive, how would you describe your contribution? The focus on contribution, on results, on why you are on the payroll, sharpens your ability to select the one or two items that are most important to you and to your company.

4. This is one of my favorites: what can you, and only you, do that, if done well, will make a real difference? Remember, you are a knowledge worker. You work with your brain, not muscle power, but mind power, and there's always one thing that only you can do that can make a real difference. If you don't do it, it won't get done, but if you do it and do it well and in a timely fashion, it can make a significant contribution to your work or to your personal life. This is where you must focus and concentrate more than anywhere else.

5. The granddaddy question in setting priorities is, what is the most valuable use of my time right now? Your ability to answer this question and apply yourself to doing only that task is the key to high levels of efficiency and effectiveness; it is the true measure of self-discipline and character.

Zero-Based Thinking

Every single day, you should be applying the law of zero-based thinking to your life and activities. This law requires continually asking yourself, is there anything that I am doing today that, knowing what I now know, I wouldn't get into again?

Ask yourself, is there anything that I am doing today that, knowing what I now know, I wouldn't get into again?

In my years of experience, I have found that every single person is doing one or more things that, knowing what they now know, they wouldn't start again. And it's impossible to organize your time and your life if you are preoccupied with doing things that you wouldn't even do if you had a chance to get out of them.

One of the fastest ways to organize your time and increase your efficiency is to stop doing things that you wouldn't do again if you had the choice. Keep asking yourself, is there anything in my life that I wouldn't get into if I had to do it over again knowing what I now know? Look at your job or career. Is it the right one for you? If it isn't, what kind of decisions do you have to make? Look at your marriage or your relationships. Would you get into them again if you had it to do over? Staying in a bad relationship after you've decided that you are unhappy is one of the greatest of all wastes of time and life. Look at your investments and your commitments of time and money. Is anything taking up a good deal of your mental, emotional, or financial resources that, knowing what you now know, you wouldn't get into?

When you identify the things that you wouldn't start up again, your next question is, how do I get out of this situation and how fast? We've never been in a situation where we know more about achieving higher levels of success, happiness, and prosperity than we do today.

* * *

In this chapter, I've touched on the ultimate luck factor: your ability to get rapid results for which people will pay you and promote you. The better you get at making a greater and greater contribution to the lives and work of other people, the more opportunities and possibilities will open up for you. You will move ahead more rapidly than the other people in your field. You will soon rise to the top of your industry, with all the rewards, recognition, and prestige that that entails. And everyone will call you lucky.

KEYS TO ACHIEVING RESULTS

1. Your most valuable asset is your reputation.
2. You can tell your true values and beliefs by the amount of your time you are willing to invest in them.
3. Use lists to manage your time.
4. Use the 80/20 rule to improve efficiency.
5. Sort your tasks using the ABCDE method.
6. Apply zero-based thinking to your activities.

10

Action Orientation

Action orientation is a hallmark of all highly successful people. It is based on organizing your life to get more done, faster, in a shorter time. It's based on the key luck factor of alertness. The more alert you are, the more likely you are to be aware of opportunities and situations that you can turn to your advantage. Many people's lives have been changed as a result of spotting a small advertisement or story in a book or magazine that gave them an idea which they acted on before anyone else and which changed their whole life.

One year Peter Thomas, a high-energy, action-oriented entrepreneur from Canada, was sitting on the beach in Hawaii at Christmastime reading *The Wall Street Journal*. He came across an advertisement seeking real estate franchisees for a new company that was starting up in Newport Beach, California. He knew a good deal about real estate, and he saw the possibility of importing this concept to Canada before anyone else. He got up from the beach, went back to the hotel, packed, caught a plane for Los Angeles, and took a taxi to the offices of Century 21. The executives of Century 21 had given very little thought to Canada. Peter Thomas was able to purchase the exclusive rights to Canada for the Century 21 real estate franchise concept. Before the dust had settled some years later, there were Century 21 offices from coast to coast in Canada, and Peter Thomas was a multimillionaire living in a penthouse suite with his yacht in the harbor below.

Thousands of people saw the same ad and turned the page without paying attention to it. But one man, because of his alertness, quickness, and action orientation, was able to take advantage of it and create a fortune.

If this story seems like a fluke that could never happen to you, you're wrong. Thousands of opportunities like this are cropping up all around you, every single day. But if you are not alert to them, they will simply pass you by.

Some years ago, a young man decided he wanted to start his own business. He attended a seminar on entrepreneurship, where he learned that 95 percent of all products manufactured in any country are never exported. He also learned that there are thousands of new, creative, innovative products being invented and marketed throughout Europe and the Far East every single year that nobody in America ever hears about. He sent away for a catalogue of European manufacturers who were looking for agents for their products in America. He knew a little bit about gardening, and he came across a description of a new high-quality, lightweight, and inexpensive wheelbarrow with a remarkably innovative design. He was convinced that there would be a market for this wheelbarrow in the United States. He immediately wrote to the company and asked them to send him a sample. They sent him a sample, which he took to a major national gardening trade show a month later. He couldn't afford his own booth, so he arranged to share a little bit of booth space with another manufacturer of garden equipment. Buyers for three major department store chains came by, saw the wheelbarrow, recognized its market potential, and placed orders with him for 64,000 units at the one trade show. By the time he had filled the orders, he was a millionaire.

The entire process took less than a year from the time he set a goal, made a decision, acted on it, and sold the 64,000 wheelbarrows, making a profit of almost $20 each.

I've worked with millionaires and multimillionaires who have limited education and limited business experience, but one thing they have all had in common is the psychological disposition to move quickly when opportunities or problems present themselves. Of course, the more you study your field and learn your skills, the more knowledgeable and aware you will be, and the easier it will be to recognize opportunities when they appear.

Move quickly when opportunities present themselves.

The Momentum Strategy of Success

Here's one of the most important luck factors of all. It is called the *momentum strategy of success*. It says that a person in motion tends to remain in motion, and it takes much less energy to keep moving than to stop and try to get into motion again. Once you get started, it's easier to keep going than to stop and then start up again. If it takes ten units of energy to get into motion, it only takes a couple of units of energy to stay in motion, but if you stop, it takes you another full ten units of energy to get going again.

You've probably had the experience of going away on vacation and coming back after a week or two. Do you remember how hard it was to get back into your job and get up to full steam again? Sometimes it takes several days. Sometimes it even takes as many days to get going again as you've been away.

Many people who stop never get going again. There is a quotation that says, on the beaches of hesitation lie the bleached bones of those who, at the moment of victory, rested, and in resting lost all. It's like keeping plates spinning. As long as the circus performer keeps applying pressure to the sticks the plates are spinning on, they keep spinning indefinitely. But if the plates are allowed to slow down below a certain speed, they fall off the stick, and the trick is over.

You must keep in continuous motion yourself. Always keep your plates spinning. Do something every day that is moving you toward your goals. Be a moving target—difficult or impossible to hit. The faster you move, the more you get done, and the more likely you are to do the right thing for the right person at the right time. Always, time is of the essence.

The Law of Flexibility

The law of flexibility is vital to luck and success. It says that you must be clear about your goal, but you must always remain flexible about the way you attain it. Flexibility is considered to be the most important psychological quality for success in a fast-changing world. You must be prepared to bend like the willow tree in front of the winds of change rather than snapping like the pine tree when the situation alters in directions that you hadn't anticipated.

A sophisticated missile, once it's programmed to its target, will move unerringly toward the target. It will continually adjust course and direction until it hits its target. No evasive action on the part of the target will be sufficient to enable it to escape destruction.

You are like a guided missile. You have the most incredible guidance mechanism imaginable. Once you are programmed toward a clear, specific, written, and measurable goal, your superconscious mind moves you unerringly over every obstacle. It gives you every lesson you need. As long as you keep in motion, you will ultimately achieve your goal, sometimes in completely unexpected ways.

The guided missile cannot adjust course or change direction until it is launched and in flight. You are the same. As long as you are in motion toward your goals and concentrating on high priorities, you will get continual feedback from your environment. It will enable you to make course corrections that will bring you unerringly to your target. But you must keep moving and moving fast.

Initiative: The Magic Ingredient

A recent study conducted by the American Management Association identified the one quality that seems to separate the most successful people from the least successful: initiative. The higher performers showed vastly greater levels of initiative than the average performers. Top people were much quicker to take responsibility and act when they saw something that needed to be done. They were much more proactive than reactive. They anticipated the importance of a particular behavior and moved quickly, usually without detailed discussion or analysis.

Here's the interesting thing: when the researchers interviewed the average managers and asked them if they felt they had initiative, they all answered in the affirmative. They all felt that they showed a good deal of initiative. So the researchers asked them to define what initiative meant for them.

The average managers described such things as answering the phone when it rang, calling up someone to remind them of a meeting or a commitment, or bringing a piece of news or information to someone else's attention. But the researchers found that the high performers considered these activities to be merely part of the job. The high performers defined initiative as something well above and beyond the call of duty: taking risks, moving out of the comfort zone, working longer hours, and doing things that the average person would not bother to do.

It's the same with you. The more initiative you show, the more you are perceived as a valuable player. When you continually seek out newer, faster, better, easier, more convenient ways to get the job done for your company and your customers, you quickly come to the attention of the people who can help you.

> The more initiative you show, the more
> you are perceived as a valuable player.

The head of Amoco Petroleum, a major oil company with a reputation for developing more reserves of oil and gas than any other one in the industry, was once asked why his company was so much more successful at this than others. He explained that the answer was simple. The other companies all had similar land leases, similar geological studies, and similar engineers and equipment. Amoco was ahead of the other companies, he said, because they drilled more holes. It was no miracle. They put down more wells, and as a result they discovered more oil.

In our studies of unemployed people searching for new jobs, we found a remarkable fact. Some quickly get back into the workplace, at good jobs with good salaries and good possibilities; others are unemployed for long periods. The people who quickly get back to work look upon job hunting as a full-time activity. They get up and start at seven or eight in the morning, and they work hard and fast all day long. They're continually reading ads, making phone calls, sending résumés, and going to interviews. But the majority of people who have been laid off, especially from jobs they'd had for a long time, pursue an average of two possible jobs per week.

Not long ago, a counselor for a group of unemployed executives noticed that at every weekly meeting, they spent the entire time complaining about their past companies and blaming their bosses for letting them go. So he suggested that next week, instead of talking about negative things, each person would share one interview experience they had had. A week later, only two of the sixteen executives showed up. When the counselor phoned around to find out why they hadn't come to the meeting, he found that none of them had had a single job interview in the last week. They had spent the entire time sitting at home watching television or hanging around the house. He recognized they were all so negative because none of them were out in the marketplace actively talking to people and pursuing new career opportunities.

The faster you move, the more energy you have, and the more experience you get. The faster you move, and the more experience you have, the better and smarter you become. The faster you move, the more bases you cover, the more people you see, and the more likely it is that you will strike oil.

Seven Keys to Productivity

Here are seven key ideas that you can use to increase your productivity, performance, and output immediately. These techniques are practiced by all the highest-performing, highest-paid people in every business.

1. Work faster; pick up the pace; move more quickly; develop a sense of urgency. Whatever you have to do, do it in real time; act on it immediately. Fast tempo is essential to success. Repeat over and over to yourself: *do it now, do it now, do it now.* You can double your output simply by resolving to walk faster, move faster, act faster, decide faster, and get on with it, whatever it is. All successful people are quick and efficient; all ineffective people delay and procrastinate. The faster you do it, the more luck you will turn out to have.

2. Work longer and harder. Most people are lazy, and they don't work very hard even when they are at work. Sustained, concentrated, applied effort is the key to high performance and productivity.

   Here's one of the paradoxes of working in an office: you can't get work done at work. You are swamped by telephone interruptions, people interruptions, meetings, unexpected emergencies, and a dozen other things that sap your time and energy and leave you at the end of the day feeling that the more you have to get done, the less you seem to do. However, one hour of uninterrupted time will enable you to do the equivalent amount of work of three hours of normal office time, where you're constantly interrupted.

So start one hour earlier, work at lunchtime, and stay an hour later. This will add three hours of uninterrupted, productive time to your day and enable you to produce the amount of work that another person would produce in nine hours. In fact, you will produce the equivalent of two people.

Office hours are not for successful people. Anyone who watches the clock has very little future in their current job or industry. Your attitude toward the clock should be that it merely keeps score and tells you how much more time you have before your next task or responsibility. Never look at the clock to see how late you can start or how soon you can quit.

Anyone who watches the clock has
very little future in their current job.

If you get up a little earlier and go to the office one hour before anyone else, you will immediately start to join the ranks of the top people in America. It's a truism in sales that if you want to talk to the top people, call before the receptionist or the secretary gets there. The top people are always in the office the earliest, sometimes by 6:00 or 7:00 a.m. On the other end of the day, if you want to get past the gatekeeper, wait until the company closes and call at 6:00 or 7:00 p.m. Very often the person who answers will be the top person in the organization. The reason he or she is the top person is because he or she gets in early and stays late.

By the way, there is no law that requires you to automatically get up from your desk at noon, walk out the door with whoever is standing there, and spend an hour eating lunch. Successful people don't do this. They make every minute count. If you take the hour between 12:00 and 1:00 p.m., close your door, put your head down, and concentrate on getting your top jobs out of the way, you'll be able to accomplish the equivalent of two or three hours of interrupted time.

The highest-paid people in America—those in the top 10 or 20 percent—work an average of fifty-nine hours per week. This means either six ten-hour days or five twelve-hour days. In my years of studying success, I've never found a person who has achieved anything worthwhile working eight hours per day. Your success will be in direct proportion to the number of hours that you put in over eight hours each day, that is, over forty hours each week. When you start working fifty, sixty, and seventy hours per week, and you use that time well by constantly working on your highest priority tasks, you will move ahead rapidly.

3. Do more important things. Since you only have a certain number of hours in each day, make sure that every minute is spent doing the most important and valuable things. Continually ask yourself, "If I had to leave town for a month and I could only do one more thing before I left, what would that be?" Whatever it is, discipline yourself to work on that and only that until it's finished.

Single-minded concentration on one task, the most important task, will put you onto a higher plane of performance. You will get more done in the same amount of time, your thinking will become crystal clear, you will activate your superconscious mind, and your life will sparkle with ideas and insights that you can use to accomplish tasks even faster. But you will only get into this zone when you work faster and harder and concentrate on high-value tasks.

You've heard it said that if you want something done, give it to a busy person. The reason is simple: A busy person is working at a higher rate of output than a person who only does it when they get around to it. The person is doing two or three times as much in the course of a day as one who is working at a slower pace or lower level of activity.

4. Work on the things that you do the best. This way, you will not only enjoy them more because of your sense of mastery, but you will also get them done faster. You make fewer mistakes. You make a more valuable contribution.

One of the best time management techniques you'll ever learn is to commit yourself to getting better at the most important things you do. Since your major rewards and recognition come from doing your most important tasks and doing them well, the better you get at those key tasks, the more rewards, recognition, and opportunity you will earn, and the more you will experience the luck that seems to be denied to those who are satisfied doing a job at a level that allows them to just get by.

5. Bunch your tasks. Do groups of similar tasks together. Return all your phone calls together; do all your telephone prospecting together; fill out all your expense accounts at the same time; write all your letters and proposals at the same time.

One of the most powerful time saving techniques is the learning curve. Learning curve theory says that the more you do of a repetitive task, the faster and more easily you perform each subsequent task. If it takes you ten minutes to do the first of a series of tasks, it will take you only nine minutes for the second task, eight minutes for the third, seven minutes for the fourth, and so on. You can get down to two minutes per task—saving 80 percent of the time it would normally take you if you did your tasks, one at a time, separately from one other.

Many people are oblivious to the learning curve. They perform a task in one area and then perform a task in another area. They never get onto the learning curve, and they never find themselves producing at high levels.

6. Do things with others. Your ability to function well as part of a team is critical to your success. When you cooperate and work effectively with others, with each person taking the part of the job that they're best suited to, you will be amazed at what you can accomplish.

Your ability to function well as part of
a team is critical to your success.

During World War II, the US government made a commitment to building Liberty ships for carrying cargo across the North Atlantic at a faster rate than they could be sunk by the German U-boats. The government created a series of industrial innovations that are still being used worldwide today. First, they reduced the time needed to build a ship from two years all the way down to forty-two days. Then, in an incredible display of teamwork, the skilled workmen got together, made a plan, and built an entire ship ready for launching in four days. They were able to build hundreds of Liberty ships because they used the learning curve, they bunched their tasks together, and they worked as a smooth, well-oiled team. Look for opportunities to apply the same principles to your work as well.

7. Simplify and streamline your work. Use the time management technique of process analysis. This entails making a list of every step in a particular process from the time you begin to the time you finish. Then go through the list of steps, and look at which ones you could simplify so you can do them faster. Identify steps that you could consolidate with other steps or jobs or that you can consolidate in a single person. Finally, look for parts of the task that you could eliminate altogether.

Time Compression by Responsibility Expansion

There's a powerful productivity improvement technique called *time compression by responsibility expansion.* Let me explain how this works. In one study of the processing of life insurance policies, the researchers discovered that it was taking six weeks from the time a policy was submitted from the field to the time it was either approved or disapproved at the head office.

The researchers took a policy and followed it through the steps involved in approval. They found that the policy went through twenty-four steps in six weeks, but the actual amount of time spent working on it was only seventeen minutes. So they reengineered the way of handling the policy. Instead of having twenty people look at it, they reduced the number of people to two. The first person would check out every single detail of the policy from beginning to end. It would then be sent to a second, more senior person who would double-check the work of the first person. Using this technique, they were able to reduce the processing time of a policy from six weeks down to twenty-four hours. Their underwriting business increased over the next year by millions of dollars.

Time is the most valuable element in business and personal life. Everyone thinks in terms of time and reducing the amount of time it takes to get a task done. People who can do things quickly because they are using the most effective time management techniques are always the most valued and most rapidly promoted people. They get the lucky breaks.

People who manage their time most effectively
are the ones who get the lucky breaks.

Energy and Enthusiasm

To be at the top of your form, to be action-oriented, fast moving, and productive, you have to have a great deal of energy and enthusiasm. Energy is a key luck factor. To be alert to the possibilities around you and have the enthusiasm that keeps you moving forward, you have to design your life so that you feel terrific about yourself most of the time.

Today we know more about what you can do or refrain from doing to enjoy higher levels of energy than we have ever known before. I'm going to give you the key factors that determine your energy levels, and I encourage you to incorporate them into your daily life and habits.

DIET

Eat the right foods in the right balance and in the right combinations. Your diet can have an inordinate impact on the amount of energy you have, how well you sleep, your health and fitness, and your performance throughout the day.

Olympic athletes have been studied extensively to find out what they eat. Even though the athletes may come from more than 100 countries, Olympic diets have been found to have three things in common. They are very easy to learn and implement.

Olympic athletes eat lots of fruit, vegetables, and whole grain foods. They eat lots of pasta and rice, which are complex carbohydrates that turn rapidly into glucose and serve as a fuel for the high-performance body and mind. The diet specialists who coach people for fitness and high energy say that because your body is 70 percent water, you should eat 70 percent water-based foods like fruits and vegetables. In addition, whole-grain products, like whole-grain bread, brown rice, bran muffins, shredded wheat, and bran flakes, provide the necessary roughage to keep your system functioning smoothly.

The second part of the high-performance Olympic diet is lean source protein. This is protein like fish, chicken with no skin, lean beef, and so on. These are lower in fat than most other foods. In fact, fat has been found to correlate with an enormous number of physical ailments and health problems. It is possible to eat a low-fat diet and immediately start losing excess pounds and gaining energy. When you combine a low-fat diet with increased amounts of fruits and vegetables and whole grain products, you will trim down quickly and feel far better about yourself.

The third part of a high-performance diet is drinking lots of water. Most people just sip water when they drink, but you need to be drinking eight eight-ounce glasses of water per day to combat the normal water loss that occurs as a result of daily activities.

Today you see more and more people today carrying water bottles around. They sip from those bottles continually. They are constantly flushing out salts, toxins, waste products, and other residues that can build up in your system and slow you down.

Today about 42 percent of Americans are obese, many of them grossly so. Being overweight is one of the fastest ways to reduce your energy level, lower your credibility to a health-conscious customer, and shorten your life.

One of your goals should be to achieve high levels of physical fitness. You can begin getting your weight and physical appearance under control by changing your diet away from fatty, sugary, salty foods toward healthy, nutritious, energy- and vitamin-rich foods. The choice is up to you.

EXERCISE

The second key ingredient to high energy is proper exercise. The best activity is aerobic exercise, which brings your heart and respiratory rate up to what is called the training zone, about 140 beats per minute (more or less, dependent upon your age), and keeps it there for twenty to thirty minutes, three times per week.

You can get all the exercise you need, for example, by walking two or three miles three to five times per week. You can get your exercise from swimming, cycling, using exercise equipment, or jogging. Your body is meant to be fully used every day. Every joint should be fully articulated. Stretch your arms, back, and legs completely. Use light weights to keep your muscles strong and supple. Most of all, you should be getting aerobic exercise on a regular basis if you want to feel and look terrific.

REST AND RECREATION

The third key to high energy is proper rest. You need seven to eight hours of sleep per night on average. You also need to take off at least one full day per week—when you don't work at all. You will find that you are most alert and creative in the two or three days following a vacation of any kind, even a two- or three-day weekend vacation.

One way to increase your alertness, energy, and productivity is to take regular miniholidays of two or three days each, as well as regular annual holidays, when you let go completely and get your mind totally off your work. In the day or two after you come back, you will have more ideas and produce more good results than you will if you work nonstop until you're exhausted and burned out.

NO SMOKING

The fourth key to excellent health and high energy is no smoking. Smoking has been correlated with thirty-two different diseases and ailments. There is no single action that you can take that is worse for your health than smoking on a regular basis. You can eliminate smoking by setting it as a goal, affirming that you are a nonsmoker, visualizing yourself as a nonsmoker, and disciplining yourself to refuse cigarettes. You can do anything you want to do if you really put your mind to it.

VITAMIN SUPPLEMENTS

The fifth key to high energy is to add regular vitamin and mineral supplements to your diet. Today's diet is deficient in key vitamins and minerals. The healthiest people regularly balance their nutritional deficiencies with high-quality vitamins and minerals. The best ones are those from natural sources, which are usually bound with chelates. They cost more, but more of the vitamins and minerals contained in them are absorbed by your body.

MENTAL HEALTH

The sixth key to high energy has to do with your mental health. It's the elimination of negative emotions, especially your expression of negatives of any kind. The more you think about or talk about the things that make you angry or unhappy, the angrier and more unhappy you become. Your negative emotions depress your mind and body; they tire you out and fatigue you. One unrestrained outburst of anger can consume as much energy as eight hours of regular work.

You can overcome your tendency to condemn and complain (which just about everyone does) by canceling out negative emotions through the law of substitution. Whenever you feel angry or upset, immediately say, *Wait. I am responsible. I am responsible. I am responsible.* It's impossible to accept responsibility for your life and to be angry at the same time.

> It's impossible to accept responsibility for your life and to be angry at the same time.

Virtually all negativity comes from anger, resentment, and blaming other people. The instant you stop blaming others and start accepting responsibility, you feel a tremendous sense of control, you feel a surge of positive energy, and you feel that you are back on top of your life.

* * *

The more you practice these health habits and focus on your goals and the things you want, the more energy and vitality you will have. The more alert and aware you will be, the more positive you will feel, and the more action-oriented you will become. It will be as though you have put your entire life into overdrive, and you'll feel yourself racing forward at a rate greater than you've ever imagined.

KEYS TO ACTION

1. Alertness is crucial to success.
2. Decisiveness is a common feature of practically all successful individuals.
3. Be clear about your goal, but be flexible in how you attain it.
4. Initiative means acting above and beyond the call of duty.
5. Use the seven keys to productivity to improve your performance.
6. Adjust your lifestyle to ensure a maximum of energy and enthusiasm.

11

Virtue, Courage, and Persistence

The Greek philosopher Aristotle, who lived in the fourth century BC, is considered perhaps the most important philosopher in Western history. In his great work the *Nicomachean Ethics*, he stated that all human behavior is purposeful. It is aimed at a goal. Everything you do, he said, you do for a reason, and behind every smaller goal, there is a larger goal that you are striving toward.

Aristotle determined that the ultimate goal for everyone is happiness. No matter what you do, your ultimate goal—beyond what you are trying to accomplish at the moment—is to achieve your own happiness. You are successful in life to the degree to which you are genuinely happy. You are a failure in life to the degree to which you cannot attain your own happiness.

Say you want to get a good job. Why? So that you can earn a good living. Why? So that you can have enough money. Why? So that you can buy a house and a car and have a nice standard of living. Why? So that you can have happy relationships and a good life with other people. Why? The final answer is always so that you can be happy.

The only difference among people is that some are better at achieving happiness than others. Some people make choices and decisions that make them unhappy and worse off. In any event, happiness is always the goal.

Aristotle did not stop there. He went on to examine the human condition and came to a remarkable conclusion: only the good can be happy, and only the virtuous can be good. This is one of the major breakthroughs in philosophy: you can only be happy if you're a good person, and you can only be a good person if you practice the virtues that are associated with goodness. In short, if you want to have a wonderful life, you must continually strive to become a better and better person. Any deviation from this course will lead you to unhappiness and dissatisfaction. Every time you act consistently with the highest virtues that you know, you feel happy and strong inside, your self-confidence and self-esteem go up, and you become more effective in your relationships and your work. A virtue is its own reward. It pays for itself in the inner feeling of pleasure and contentment that you have when you live consistently with the very best that you know.

Character is the greatest of all luck factors. I've already emphasized that you inevitably attract the people, circumstances, ideas, opportunities, and resources that are in harmony with your dominant thoughts. You can never have on the outside what you do not deserve by right of the consciousness that you have built on the inside. By the law of correspondence, your outer world is always a reflection of your inner world. If you want to change your outer world, you must reprogram your subconscious mind, your world of values, beliefs, and inner convictions, so that the person you are inside is the exact mental equivalent of the life you want to enjoy on the outside.

Character is the greatest of all luck factors.

You're probably reading this book because you want to be happier and more successful, with better relationships, more money, and greater self-expression. You want to have a great life. You are superior to the average person because you are willing to constantly learn more about how you can become better and better. But what is success?

The Chief Rewards of Success

Some years ago, Gallup interviewed 1,500 members of Who's Who in America. These are among the most prestigious of all living Americans—company presidents, leading politicians, Nobel Prize winners, and others who have made significant contributions to American life. The pollsters asked these highly successful men and women what they considered to be the chief rewards of success. The first four rewards of success that virtually all of them gave might surprise you.

1. They felt they had earned the respect of their parents.
2. They felt they had earned the respect of their spouses and their children.
3. They felt they had earned the respect of their peers and colleagues.

4. They felt that what they were doing was making a difference in the lives of other people.

The fifth ingredient of success was that these individuals no longer worried about money, even though many of them were not particularly wealthy. They had simply reached a point where it didn't matter that much in contrast to the work they were doing.

Respect and Reputation

When you think of success in your own life, you will find that it is closely tied to the respect that you get from the people you respect. Almost everything you do is done or not done with a view toward how other people will think of you and react.

As I've said, your reputation is your greatest asset. It can be defined as how people think and talk about you when you're not there. As you know from your own experience, when people talk about you in either positive or negative terms and you find out about it later, it has a major impact on your thinking and your emotions, positive or negative.

Superior individuals are always thinking about how a particular decision or behavior will be evaluated by others. They are concerned not only about doing the right thing, but about doing what appears to be the right thing from the perspective of others. Because of the law of attraction, as you develop your character and live more and more by the highest and best virtues that you know, you will become a happier person. You'll also attract into your life other men and women of quality and character.

Aristotle also observed that the entire purpose of education is to inculcate the key virtues in young people so that they would be guaranteed a happy, successful life when they grew up. He knew, as you do, that everything in life is relationships. No one lives on an island unto himself. Everything we do involves others in some way, and there is no more fundamental statement about who you really are than the description of your character. But what if your education has been deficient? What if you have grown up without being trained in the essential virtues?

Aristotle pointed out that a virtue is a practice, not a simple feeling or belief. Again, it is not what you hope, wish, or intend, but what you do that counts. Aristotle said that if you do not have a virtue that you desire to have, you can develop it in yourself by practicing the virtue in every circumstance where it is called for. You can act as if you already have the virtue that you desire. The law of reversibility says that you can act your way into feeling and believing something that you sincerely desire to feel or believe. You can take complete charge of the development of your character and become a superior person by deciding that you will walk, talk, act, and think consistently with the highest and best values that you know.

The law of concentration says that whatever you dwell upon grows. You can use this powerful law to shape your character by dwelling upon a virtue that you want to be known and respected for.

Integrity is the core virtue. The dictionary definition of *integrity* includes oneness, wholeness, perfection, without blemish or fault. As you meditate on the quality of integrity and what it means to be a person of integrity, you can think of other people—those around you or historical characters—who are known and respected for their integrity.

Integrity is the core virtue.

Do you remember that nickname of Abraham Lincoln? It was Honest Abe. From the time he was a young man, working in a store and walking miles to return a couple of pennies that he had overcharged a woman, he was developing a reputation for impeccable honesty. His reputation was so strong that he was nominated to be the presidential candidate of the then new Republican party in 1860. The strength of his character carried the convention and made him one of America's most revered and respected presidents.

The more you dwell on a virtue such as integrity, the more its implications soak into your subconscious mind. The more they do, the more likely you are to act as a person of integrity. As you develop a greater reputation for integrity, more and more people will like and trust you and want to be associated with you. Doors will open. You'll start to experience luck that people with weaker characters never seem to enjoy.

Trust and Truthfulness

Political scientist Francis Fukuyama wrote a book called *Trust: The Social Virtues and the Creation of Prosperity*. It discusses various nations over the centuries and concludes that high-trust nations are highly prosperous, whereas low-trust nations have low levels of prosperity and development. The greater the level of trust amongst the people in the business community in any nation, the greater the amount of economic activity, growth, development, and prosperity. The lower the level of trust, the higher the level of corruption and dishonesty will be, and the more cautious anyone will be about investing with anyone else.

It's the same with relationships. The glue that holds a relationship together is trust. It's impossible to proceed in a relationship unless we trust and feel confident about the other person. All good friendships and all strong families are based on trust. And in companies—which are larger business families—trust is the fundamental ingredient that determines the success and prosperity of the enterprise.

The best companies to work for have a high-trust environment. Everyone in the company, at every level, trusts and believes that what other people say is true. In almost every company of value, telling a lie can be a sufficient reason for losing your job. Americans in general place an enormous emphasis on trust. It is a fundamental ingredient that holds our society together, from top to bottom.

The ultimate expression of trust is truthfulness. Your best friends and closest associates will always be those who tell you the truth. The willingness to be absolutely truthful with yourself and others is the critical mark of character. If integrity is the core quality of character, truthfulness is its most obvious expression.

Shakespeare wrote, "This above all, to thine own self be true, / And it must follow, as the night the day, / Thou canst not then be false to any man." You must always be absolutely true to yourself. This means being true to the best that is in you. It also means that you always do your best in every situation, especially at work, where people are counting on you. If the inner expression of integrity is truth, its outer expression is quality work and quality behavior under all circumstances.

In his researches, psychologist Abraham Maslow found that the most fully integrated people were extremely objective and truthful about themselves, their strengths and weaknesses, and their situations. They never tried to convince themselves of things that weren't true. They lived in truth with themselves; as a result, they were able to live in truth with others.

Refuse to play games with yourself. Refuse to pretend or wish or hope that something is not true when in your heart, you know it is. Refuse to compromise your integrity for any reason. As Ralph Waldo Emerson once wrote, "Nothing at last is sacred but the integrity of your own mind." This means living in truth with everyone around you. You state your truth simply and honestly; you do not stay in relationships that are wrong for you or do things that you do not agree with or believe in; you don't say things that are not honest and sincere expressions of your true beliefs. You adamantly insist on living in truth in every aspect of your life.

"Nothing at last is sacred but the integrity of your own mind."
—*Ralph Waldo Emerson*

The roots of self-esteem and self-confidence are deep within your character. The more you practice impeccable integrity, the greater self-confidence you have, and the more you like and respect yourself. The more you like and respect others, the more they will like and respect you. It all begins with your own inner attitudes of mind, with your own deepest values, beliefs, and convictions. Your external success is determined by your adamant internal insistence on remaining true to the best you know. Integrity is the value that guarantees all the others.

Self-Discipline: The Iron Quality

The foundation of integrity is self-discipline. Elbert Hubbard, one of the great writers of the early twentieth century, wrote that self-discipline is the ability to make yourself do what you should do, when you should do it, whether you feel like it or not.

Self-discipline is the iron quality of character. It will largely determine your success or failure in everything you do. Another way of saying self-discipline is self-control, self-mastery. You know that you only feel good about yourself to the degree to which you feel you are in control of your own life. When you make clear, unequivocal decisions to do a particular thing, and then you discipline yourself to do it, even when you don't feel like it, you feel terrific about yourself.

There's a direct correlation between self-discipline and self-esteem. The more you discipline yourself to do the things that are the best for you, the more you like and respect yourself, and the more you like and respect yourself, the more capable you are of disciplining yourself to do the things that you know you should do.

Aristotle said that you can develop any quality in solitude, except character. You can only develop character through active involvement with others. You are where you are and what you are today because of the choices and decisions that you have made in the past. You have either thought carefully, making decisions based on good information and good judgment, or you have not.

Whatever choices and decisions you made in the past, that was then, and this is now. Every day, every week, every month, you evolve and grow. As a child, you made decisions that you would never think of making as an adult. You made decisions last year that, knowing what you now know, you wouldn't make now. When you made them, you were that particular person, but today you're different. Don't be hung up on the mistakes you've made in the past. The person who made those mistakes was an earlier version of yourself. Today you can make new choices and new decisions based on your ever growing storehouse of knowledge and experience. You can put your hands on the wheel of your own future and turn it in whatever direction you want to go.

Don't be hung up on the mistakes you've made in the past.

The E Factor

Why doesn't everyone live a life of high character? Why doesn't everyone practice the virtues of integrity and truthfulness, especially since they are so closely correlated with success and happiness?

The answer is contained in what I call the *expediency factor,* or the *E factor.* It is the primary reason for failure. Only when you understand this factor can you counteract it. It is based on the fundamental flaws or weaknesses in human character.

There are many elements of human nature, but I'll just describe the basic seven. Any one of these, improperly controlled and directed, is enough to cause a person to fail. Most people have all seven of them functioning at the same time, and they therefore achieve at very low levels.

Laziness. You always attempt to conserve energy in accomplishing any task. The reason for this is that your time and your energy represent your life, and you place a value on your life. You are psychologically engineered so that you cannot consciously choose a harder way to do something if you can see an easier way. This means that, for better or for worse, you and everyone else are lazy.

Now there's nothing wrong with laziness, if it's directed constructively toward finding easier ways to accomplish the same task. The history of human advancement has lain in men and women applying their creativity to achieve the same goals with a lower expenditure of effort and energy. But when people seek easy ways that end up being counterproductive and even hurtful, laziness becomes a bad quality.

Greed. Everyone prefers more to less. If I were to offer you $5 or $10 for the same apple, you would choose $10. This is normal, natural, and healthy. All human beings prefer more to less, all else being equal. This means that everyone is greedy. Greediness is neither positive or negative. If is directed toward improving your life and increasing the well-being of yourself and others, it can be a positive influence. If it is aimed at getting something for nothing, or something that a person doesn't deserve, it can be destructive. The way that greed is applied determines whether it is a good or bad quality.

Selfishness. Everyone thinks and feels for themselves. Only you can feel your own happiness, your own dissatisfaction, your own hunger, thirst, contentment, or discontentment. No one can feel these feelings for you or decide for you what is best in these areas. And you always decide based on what you feel is best for you. This simply means that you are selfish, or at any rate self-centered. When you go to a buffet, only you can determine the ideal mixture of foods for your appetite and palate.

Again, there's nothing wrong with being selfish. It's just a fact of nature, like being lazy or greedy. A minister working in a rescue mission can be totally selfish in satisfying his deepest needs by helping as many people as he can. He can be lazy, greedy, and selfish in a healthy and constructive way.

Ambition. Every act that we engage in is to somehow improve our situation over what it would have been if we hadn't acted in the first place. Everyone seeks improvement of some kind in everything they say or do, consciously or unconsciously. This means that everyone is ambitious. Everyone wants to improve their life, work, relationships, health, or financial status. The opposite of ambition would be indifference or complacency—to be completely satisfied and not care at all whether your life gotten better or worse.

Ambition is a very healthy quality and is the great stimulus to overcoming obstacles and achieving goals that no one might have believed possible. Of course, if a person's ambition causes them to engage in dishonest or hurtful behaviors, then ambition becomes a negative quality. But in and of itself, it is neither positive or negative. As with all qualities of human nature, it is only the way that ambition is expressed that places a value upon it.

Ignorance. Nobody can ever know everything there is to know about anything. No matter how much you learn, every decision you make is based on a speculation of some kind. Because you cannot know all the facts, you can never be guaranteed that your action will bring about the results that you desire. This means that everyone is ignorant to a certain degree. Some people are more so than others, but everyone is ignorant in that no one can ever know everything there is to know, even about their area of specialization. The drive to know, to find out, to minimize risk by increasing the amount of available knowledge, is the primary reason the totality of human knowledge is doubling so rapidly today. More people are generating more information than in all of previous human history, and the rate is accelerating. This is because we intuitively recognize that we are all ignorant to some degree.

Vanity. People take pride in themselves, their appearance, accomplishments, family, work, and possessions. People like to look good and be thought well of by others. This means that everyone is vain to a certain degree. The opposite of vanity would be total indifference to how one appears. Vanity is a good thing. It leads us to strive for beauty, health, wealth, and success. Vanity is the driving force behind industries such as clothing, furniture, homewares, automobiles, cosmetics, entertainment, and sports, even the desire to start and build successful enterprises. It is also the driving force behind political activity. It exerts an inordinate influence on all your decisions.

Impatience. Everyone prefers sooner to later. Everyone wants things done now rather than at a later date. If I offered you $100 and I could give it to you now or one year from now, you would choose to have it immediately. This is normal and natural. This is just human nature. Why is this? Simple. You value your life, and your life is made up of time. Because the future is a speculation, if you can have a reward or benefit sooner, you will always prefer to have it now rather than later.

Our entire society is driven by consumers' desires to have the things they want faster, newer, and better. Every company is driven by the need for speed: to service customers faster and better than their competitors. According to Moore's law, improvements in computer design double information processing speed every eighteen months, and the cost of processing information drops in half. The speed of technology is picking up because of this incredible impatience on the part of human beings.

So what do we have? The basic person, including you, is lazy, greedy, selfish, ambitious, ignorant, vain, and impatient. The average person therefore is *expedient.* They constantly seek the fastest and easiest way to get the things they want immediately, with little or no concern for secondary consequences.

This is the E factor. The only break on its runaway impulses is self-discipline, self-restraint, and self-mastery—a return to the virtues and values and an adamant insistence on doing only the right thing and thinking it through in advance. The opposite of the E factor is the practice of the great virtues that are associated with character and with superior people.

The Great Virtues

Let's look at some of these virtues. You know that integrity is the key virtue, the one that guarantees all the others. Your integrity determines how firmly you live by what you know to be right and true.

Another extremely important virtue is responsibility. When you accept responsibility, you accept that you are the primary creative force in your own life. You are where you are and what you are because of your own thoughts and behaviors. You say continually, *I am responsible. If it's to be, it's up to me.* When you adopt the virtue of responsibility, you stop blaming other people and making excuses. You never complain, never explain. You take complete charge of your life, and you accept responsibility, not only for yourself, but for all those who look up to you and depend upon you.

When you accept responsibility, you accept that you
are the primary creative force in your own life.

Compassion is one of the greatest virtues. It enables you to be more patient, tolerant, understanding, and sympathetic toward others who are unhappy or less fortunate. Instead of trying constantly to get the things you want, you put yourself into the situation of others who are struggling; you keep reminding yourself, *There but for the grace of God go I.* The most developed individuals have been ones of great compassion. The more compassionate you are toward the less fortunate, the better a person you become. You recognize that you have been extremely fortunate to come so far, and you withhold judgment on those who may still have a long way to come.

Kindness is another great virtue. It's been said that you can never be too kind or too fair. Everyone you meet is carrying a heavy load. When you go through your day expressing kindness and courtesy to everyone you meet, you help alleviate their burdens. You leave a feeling of warmth and good cheer behind you.

When you express compassion and kindness and take responsibility, you feel better about yourself, you become a better person, you reprogram your subconscious mind, and you change your character in a healthy way.

Friendship is another wonderful virtue. You know that to have a friend, you must be a friend. You can make more friends in a few weeks by striving to be a good friend to others than you could in years trying to get people to like you. Dale Carnegie, author of *How to Win Friends and Influence People*, wrote that the best way to build friendly relationships is to become genuinely interested in others. You can overcome any shyness or insecurity by forgetting about yourself and simply asking questions of the other person: What sort of work do you do? How did you get into that field anyway? How is everything going for you? Once you've asked these questions, listen quietly and attentively to the answers, without interrupting. Nod, smile, and pay attention. The more you get out of yourself and focus your attention on others, the better you will feel about yourself, and the better others will feel about you.

These positive feelings become self-reinforcing. The more you engage in behaviors that are intrinsically rewarding, the more you program them into your personality and make them permanent parts of your character.

Gentleness is another virtue that you can cultivate. Only the strong can be gentle. People who are rough and indifferent toward others are usually weak and insincere, with low levels of self-esteem and high feelings of insecurity. When you are gentle, patient, tolerant, kind, and compassionate to others, no matter what the circumstances, you become a better person inside. You become more respected and admired, especially when you practice these qualities with your spouse and children, your friends, and your employees. Great men and women are often among the kindest and gentlest people that you'll ever meet.

The greatest of all goals is peace of mind. It is the true measure of how well you are doing. When you set peace of mind as your goal and organize your life around it, you are much less likely to make mistakes. Peace of mind only comes when you are living consistently with the highest values, when you know that you are being impeccably honest with yourself and others. Peace of mind comes when you listen to the still, small voice within you. You trust your intuition. You go with the flow of your own nature. You do what you know to be right and good and true. Then you attract people and opportunities that enable you to make more progress in a couple of years than many people make in a lifetime.

The greatest of all goals is peace of mind.

Some of the most important luck factors are courage, self-confidence, boldness, and the willingness to move forward toward your goals with no guarantees of success. With these characteristics, you can do virtually anything; without them, none of the other qualities will help you much. Fear and doubt always have been and always will be your deadliest enemies. They have done more to sabotage the possibilities of individuals than any other force in human personality. It's not what is going on around you, but what is going on within you that determines everything you are and everything you accomplish. Developing courage and resolution are the keys to your putting your entire life into high gear.

The law of willingness says that to succeed, you must be willing to do whatever it takes to achieve your goal. Of course, this means within the law and within reason. You never do anything that is illegal or immoral, nor do you jump out of airplanes without a parachute. Within these boundaries, willingness is one of the most important of all luck factors.

Many people, when they set a goal for themselves, are willing to do *almost* everything that it takes to achieve it, but this is not enough. You must be so committed to your goal that you are willing to pay any price, go any distance, and make any sacrifice. Do you want to be financially independent? Do you want to be rich? Do you want to be a millionaire over the course of your working lifetime? There are no obstacles stopping you from achieving your financial goals. Millions of men and women have achieved all of those goals, starting from nothing and many times deeply in debt, and so can you. The only question is, how badly do you want it?

There are no obstacles stopping you
from achieving your financial goals.

Once you've decided exactly what you want, you can activate the law of courage to increase your luck. This law says that if you move boldly in the direction of your goals, unseen forces will come to your aid. Many people hesitate or quit because they can't see how they're going to get from where they are to where they want to go. They don't realize that a journey of a thousand leagues begins with a single step. Only when you step out in faith and act boldly in the direction of your dreams do things really begin to happen for you.

Aristotle defined courage as a mean between recklessness on the one extreme and cowardliness on the other. Courage sits right in the middle. He observed that the way to develop courage is by practicing it in every situation where it is required.

The Acquisition of Fear

There's only one good thing about the fears that hold you back: they are all learned. You are not born with any fears. When you come into the world, you, like every other child, have two wonderful qualities. First, you are unafraid. The infant has no natural fears (except for the fears of falling and loud noises, which are physical). Second, you are completely spontaneous. Infants express themselves completely, without any thought or concern about what anyone else says or thinks.

As you grow up, your parents and the people around you instill the fears that hold you back for the rest of your life. When you explore the world around you, they tell you things like *stop, get away from there, don't touch that, put that down, get out of there,* and— perhaps the most powerful negative word of all—*no.* Whenever you try to touch, taste, or smell something, there's always someone telling you to stop; it's too dangerous; you're too small.

As a result, you soon develop the unconscious belief that you *are* too small, weak, and inadequate. You believe that you're not good enough. Soon you develop the first traces of the fear of failure, expressed in the words *I can't, I can't, I can't.*

When you become an adult, you take over this negative reinforcement process. Whenever something new or challenging comes up, you say, *I can't do that, I'm not smart enough, I'm not creative enough, I'm not educated enough, I'm not outgoing enough.* Your first reaction to a new opportunity is to come up with a reason why it's not possible for you.

More than once in this book, I have asked, do you want to be financially independent? If you're not careful, you will go to work as a prosecutor arguing against yourself. You will immediately think up all the reasons why it's not possible for you. As Henry Ford once said, if you believe you can do a thing, or you believe you can't, in either case you're probably right.

The second fear that you develop as a result of childhood conditioning is the fear of rejection. This comes about when your parents make their love for you conditional upon your behavior. If they criticize and disapprove of you because you do or don't do certain things, you learn very early to adjust your behavior so that you're always trying to do what you think they want and approve of. If you're not careful, when you grow up, you can become hypersensitive to the opinions and approval of others. Some people are so traumatized by early childhood experiences that they cannot make a decision in adult life that they think anyone around them (or even people they don't know) might disapprove of.

The greatest single obstacle to people starting their own businesses is the fear of disapproval and ridicule. Rather than having someone else not like them or not admire them, they'd rather do nothing at all. When you do nothing at all, you accomplish nothing at all, as well. As hockey player Wayne Gretzky once said, you miss 100% of the shots you don't take.

The fear of rejection is characterized by the feeling *I have to, I have to, I have to.* It's the compulsive feeling that you have to do things that others will approve of and cannot do anything that others may disapprove of.

Mild fears of failure and rejection are healthy: they can drive you to succeed. Mild feelings of inadequacy and inferiority can drive you to do the things and become the person that others will admire and respect. In this case, they act as a positive stimulus to constructive behavior. Fears of rejection, when they're expressed as a valid consideration for others, can be very healthy. The desire to be liked and accepted lies at the basis of our respect for law, courtesy, and the social norms that make civilized life possible. The Greeks had a famous saying: moderation in all things. There's nothing wrong with moderation in fears, as long as they don't slam on the brakes of your own potential (which unfortunately is the case for most people).

The way to get over the fear of failure is, whenever you think of something that is making you tense or uneasy, to cancel it out by using the law of substitution and repeating the words *I can do it, I can do it, I can do it.*

To overcome the fear of rejection, repeat to yourself, *I don't have to, I don't have to, I don't have to.* When you tell yourself you don't have to do anything that you don't want to do and you can do anything that you do want to do, you take full control of your mind and emotions, both consciously and subconsciously. The more you act boldly and move in the direction of your dreams, the more the law of attraction goes to work for you. The more confident and optimistic you become, the more your superconscious mind adjusts your thoughts and behaviors—and the world around you—so that you experience incidents of serendipity and synchronicity over and over.

Earlier I talked about the importance of dreaming big dreams. Here's the greatest question of all for blasting through the fears that hold you back: what one great thing would you dare to dream if you knew you could not fail? If you knew you had no limitations at all? If you were absolutely guaranteed of success, what one big goal would you set for yourself?

> What one great thing would you dare to
> dream if you knew you could not fail?

Almost everyone knows the answer to this question as soon as they hear it. But the instant you define the answer, your fears surge in on you from all sides like a mob of subconscious demons, arousing doubts and anxieties and undermining your confidence.

Here's a good way to test the mental obstacles that you've used to hold yourself back. Ask yourself, is there anyone else who has experienced the same limitations that I have but who has gone on to be successful anyway? This question forces you to be honest with yourself. It forces you to stop playing games with your own head. Whatever your favorite excuse is, you can be absolutely sure that there are thousands of people who have had it far worse than you could ever dream of having it, yet who have gone on to accomplish wonderful things and make significant contributions to their lives, families, and communities. So what's holding you back?

Learned Helplessness

Psychologists have identified two major factors that cause you to be afraid far more than is justified by the facts. The first, which is deeply rooted in the fear of failure, is the feeling of learned helplessness. In his book *Learned Optimism*, psychologist Martin Seligman explains that perhaps 80 percent or more of our population has this feeling to one degree or another. It is the feeling that you are helpless, that there's nothing that you can do. It's manifested in continually using the words *I can't, I can't.*

Abraham Maslow said that the history of the human race is the story of men and women selling themselves short. You settle for far less than is possible for you because you become unconsciously convinced that there's very little that you can do to change things. However, this is not really true. You can bring about dramatic changes—sometimes very quickly—by practicing the lessons of luck we've talked about here.

In reality, the only limitations on your abilities are your imagination and your desire. Remember Napoleon Hill's famous words: "Whatever the mind of man can conceive and believe, it can achieve." If there's any goal that you can clearly define and plan, you almost certainly have the inborn capabilities and talents to achieve it. Your ability to articulate and define something that you really want means that you have the ability to attain it, as long as you want it long enough and hard enough.

The Comfort Zone

The second fear that holds people back from great success is the comfort zone. We're all creatures of habit, and we tend to stick by it, even if we're not particularly happy with the results.

The law of habit says that in the absence of a clear decision on your part, or some external stimulus, you will keep on acting in the same way indefinitely. The law of habit is the same as the law of inertia first articulated by Sir Isaac Newton. He said that a body in motion tends to remain in motion, unless acted upon by an external force. This law, applied to you, says that you will continue to do the same things, associate with the same people, earn the same amount of money, and enjoy the same level of accomplishment unless you clearly decide to change your situation or something happens to you that forces you to change, that forces you out of your comfort zone.

This is why losing a job, the breakdown of a marriage, or the loss of all your money can actually be a good thing. It can jar you out of your complacency and kick you out of your comfort zone. It can wake you up to other directions that you can go in.

No matter what happens to you, force yourself to be future-oriented. Instead of dwelling on your past problems, throw your mind forward and ask, *What do I do from here? What's the next step?* And especially, *what can I learn from this situation that will help me to be stronger and better in the future?*

Act As If It Were Impossible to Fail

The law of assumption was best summed up by the writer Dorothea Brande, who concluded that it was the greatest of all secrets of success: whatever you sincerely desire, act as if it were impossible to fail, and it shall be.

Remember, you can only tell what you truly believe and value by looking at the way you act, the decisions and choices you make, and the behaviors you engage in. Anyone can tell your real goals and values simply by looking at what you do every day. If a person says that he wants to be happy, healthy, and financially independent but eats too much, exercises too little, seldom reads, and spends his evening watching television, he is telling the world what he really wants. He wants to have an easy, undisciplined life, characterized by wasted time and empty hours of brainless entertainment. Whatever a person sows, that is what he will reap.

Everyone is afraid. You are afraid, I am afraid, and everyone you meet is afraid. As a result of our conditioning, we all grow up with an entire list of fears. They sometimes help us but mostly hurt us or hold us back.

If everyone is afraid, what is the difference between the brave person and the coward? The answer is simple. The brave person is the person who acts in spite of his fears. The coward is the person who allows his fears to overwhelm him. Ralph Waldo Emerson once wrote that the most important lesson he ever learned was this: do the thing you fear, and the death of fear is certain.

Superior individuals make a habit of confronting their fears. When you can identify a fear and move toward it, the fear diminishes and loses its hold over you. But if you back away, the fear grows and grows until it dominates your life.

The law of habit says that whatever you do over and over again becomes a new habit. If you make a habit of confronting your fears, of doing the thing you fear, acting as if you had no fears at all in any difficult situation, your fears diminish and your courage increases. Soon you will reach the point where you are virtually unafraid of anything. What great goals would you set for yourself if you had no fears at all?

The Worry Buster

Here's a great exercise. Take your dream list and use the worry buster method on each of your dreams, goals, and fantasies. Write down all of them in a column on the left-hand side of the page. Draw a line down the center of the page, and in the right-hand column opposite your goals, write out the worst possible thing that could happen if you immediately took action toward that goal. In almost every case, you'll find the worst possible consequence will not be as serious as you might imagine.

One symptom of subconscious fears is worry. Worry is a sustained form of fear caused by indecision and self-doubt. It is a form of negative imagination. It is thinking about, emotionalizing, and imagining exactly the things that you don't want to happen.

The law of attraction is neutral. Your mind, especially your superconscious mind, is extraordinarily powerful, but it draws into your life exactly the things that you most emotionalize and think about. People who worry about money have money problems. People who are critical, demanding, and impatient always seem to have relationship problems. People who are constantly looking for fast, easy ways to get their jobs done without putting their whole hearts into their responsibilities always have problems at work.

Your mind is extraordinarily powerful. It draws into your life the things that you most emotionalize and think about.

When you worry, you attract into your life more of the things that you're worrying about. This is why you must be adamant about thinking, talking about, and imagining only the things you want. You must absolutely refuse to dwell upon the things that you don't want. This is one of the greatest of all tests of character and self-control. It is the key component of success and happiness.

The Mastery of Courage

Your willingness to take risks, move out of your comfort zone, break the bonds of learned helplessness, and commit yourself completely to the accomplishment of worthwhile goals with no guarantees of success is an extremely important luck factor. How do you develop the quality of courage? Here are three steps, which you can use over and over.

First, when you think of a situation that makes you afraid, identify the worst possible thing that could happen as the result of that situation. Once you've identified it, resolve to accept it should it occur. Then you can stop worrying about it and put it out of your mind. Once you've done this, you can think of the things you can do to ensure that it won't happen. Once you've identified the worst possible thing that can happen in any situation, your fears and worries tend to evaporate; your mind becomes calm and clear. You can focus all of your energies and enthusiasm on success rather than failure.

Years ago, when I was in competitive karate, I learned an interesting technique from one of the top karate masters in the world. I found that if you move forward in a karate match, even half an inch at a time, your opponent will move backward to keep the relative distance the same between you. Because I was moving forward, 100 percent of my energy and attention were forward. Because my opponent was moving backward, as much as half of his energy was on where he was going, toward the edge of the mat. I was able to do very well in several national championship matches because I always moved forward, even against better opponents. Focusing 100 percent of your energies forward gives you that critical edge that can make all the difference between success and failure.

Another way to build up your courage and diminish your fears is to identify all the rewards you will enjoy as a result of achieving your goals. Write them all down. Friedrich Nietzsche, the German philosopher, once wrote, "He who has a why to live for can bear almost any how." The more reasons you have for achieving your goals, the more rewards you can imagine, the more power and energy you will have. Remember, you can only think about one thing at a time. If you're thinking about the rewards of success, you cannot simultaneously think about the penalties of failure. The more you think about what you want, the stronger and more powerful you become. And the more powerful you become, the more courage you develop, until you reach the point where you're not afraid of anything. You will start to become unstoppable in your movement toward your goals.

"He who has a why to live for can bear almost any how."
—*Friedrich Nietzsche*

The Power of Persistence

If the first part of courage is the willingness to begin, act in faith, and move forward towards your goals with no guarantee of success, the second part is the willingness to endure and persist. Sometimes your only advantage is that you have made a firm decision that you will never give up. In any competitive situation, the person who is the most resolute and determined is usually the one who will win. People usually fail not because they lack ability or opportunities but because they lack inner strength and persistence in the face of obstacles.

As soon as you set a big goal for yourself, it will be as if your ship of life has hit a storm. You will go into a squall, and you will be tossed and turned by a series of unexpected reverses and difficulties. When you set new big, challenging goals, your superconscious triggers changes in the world around you, all of which have only one thing in common: they are meant to bring you the experiences and opportunities you need to perform at the new high standard you have set for yourself.

Here are two powerful questions that you can use to turn failure into success and increase your persistence in the face of adversity. I call these the golden questions. I learned them from a self-made millionaire, and I've taught them to many people who have used them to become self-made millionaires as well.

The first question, no matter what happens, is, *What did I do right?* Carefully analyze every single thing that you did right in that situation. Even if it turned out to be a disaster, you did certain things that were worthwhile, productive, and worth repeating.

Then ask yourself the second question: *What would I do differently if I had this situation to do over again?* This forces you to think about the lessons in this situation. It forces you to think toward the future and what you can do rather than toward the past and what has happened.

Both of these questions require positive answers that enable you to extract the maximum value out of every situation. They enable you to keep your mind positive, focused, and forward-oriented. They enable you to learn and grow at a rapid rate. If you ask these two questions, after every situation, you will learn and grow more in the next month than someone else might learn in two or three years.

If you work with other people, you should conduct an exercise with these questions on a regular basis. You will be astonished at the insights that will help you to move ahead faster and will cause you to experience luck beyond your imagination.

One of my favorite quotes is from Phil Knight of Nike shoes. He said that you only have to succeed the last time. You can fail over and over again, but all it takes is one big success—which is virtually inevitable if you persist—and it wipes out all previous failures. No one ever accomplishes greatly without having passed the persistence test. It's like an exam that you must take over and over again. You can only advance as you develop ever higher levels of persistence. Most people achieve their greatest successes one step beyond where anyone else would have quit. But this person, who had resolved never to give up until he achieved his goal, kept on keeping on and finally broke through.

Sometimes your greatest failure can be the springboard to your greatest success. Sometimes the complete collapse of an idea or an enterprise is the final piece of the jigsaw puzzle that enables you to make the decision that achieves financial independence for you.

Persistence versus Stubbornness

By the way, there is a difference between persistence and stubbornness. Persistence is persevering toward a clear goal while remaining flexible regarding the means of attaining it. You always keep your eye on the ball. You always know where you're going. But you are willing to chop and change and try a variety of different ways to get there, and you never give up.

Stubbornness, on the other hand, is flying in the face of the facts. You are trying to make something work that is obviously unworkable. The evidence against you is overwhelming. You are simply not being realistic or honest about yourself and the situation.

> Persistence is persevering toward a clear goal.
> Stubbornness is flying in the face of the facts.

You must think about the difference between persistence and stubbornness on a regular basis, and make sure that it is persistence that you are engaging in and not stubbornness.

The more you persist, the more you believe in yourself, and the more you believe in yourself, the more you persist. Your persistence is your measure of how much you believe in yourself. You can increase your conviction of ultimate success simply by acting as if your success were ultimately guaranteed as long as you keep going. You become unstoppable by refusing to stop. When you develop a consistent action orientation and you apply the momentum strategy to your activities, you become like a force of nature, like a flash flood or a glacier moving inexorably in a particular direction. You become stronger and more optimistic, more resolute, and eventually unstoppable.

When you develop the twin qualities of courage and persistence, you will begin to experience luck in ways that you never thought possible before. The more you practice courage and persistence, the better and stronger you become. If the first key to success is get-to-it-tiveness, the second part of success is stick-to-it-tiveness. Once you launch towards your goal, you simply resolve that you will keep putting one foot in front of the other until you finally get there.

A Summary of Success

Throughout this book, I've explained that luck is predictable. Success and happiness are not accidents. Everything that happens to you happens to you for a good reason. People are where and what they are because of themselves, and especially because of the things they think about most of the time. The great secret of success is that there are no secrets of success.

From the beginning of recorded history, the reasons for success have been discovered and rediscovered over and over again. They are:

1. Be absolutely clear about the things you want and the person you want to become.
2. Think and talk continually about only those things. Refuse to think, talk, or worry about things that you don't want.

3. Learn everything that you possibly can to excel at what you do. Develop your skills and resolve to be among the top 10 percent in your field. This will help you more than anything else.

4. Become a totally positive person, so that people like you and want to be around you and help you.

5. Develop a strategy for expanding your network of contacts and relationships. The more people who know you and like you, the more doors they will open for you.

6. Make a habit of saving your money. Start with 1 percent and then eventually build up to 10, 20, and even 30 percent. A person with money in the bank attracts more opportunities and good luck than a person who is broke.

7. Unlock your inborn creativity. You are a potential genius. There is no problem that you cannot solve and no goal that you cannot achieve by applying the incredible power of your mind.

8. Continually focus on results, on the most valuable use of your time, every minute of every day.

9. Action orientation is the essential quality of all successful people. Get going, get busy, move fast, develop a sense of urgency, and stay in perpetual motion in the direction of your aspirations.

10. Develop your character. The finer a person you become on the inside, the more wonderful life you will have on the outside.

11. Finally, have the courage to begin and the persistence to endure.

When you combine all of these factors, you become a totally positive, future-focused, energetic, likable, talented, skilled, intelligent, and optimistic human being. You become unstoppable, and you begin to have lucky experiences in every area of your life, which will enable you to achieve every goal that you can ever set. Later on, when people say you are lucky, you can smile humbly and talk about how fortunate you've been and how grateful you feel for it. But in your heart, you will know it wasn't luck at all. You did it all by yourself.

KEYS TO DEVELOPING VIRTUE

1. The ultimate goal for everyone is happiness.
2. You can only be happy if you're a good person. You can only be a good person if you acquire virtue.
3. Integrity is the core virtue.
4. Being true to yourself means being true to the best that is in you.
5. The E factor is the primary reason for failure. Its antidote is self-discipline.
6. To achieve more and greater things, get out of your comfort zone.
7. Have the courage to begin and the persistence to endure.

CPSIA information can be obtained
at www.ICGtesting.com
Printed in the USA
JSHW010503300623
43774JS00001B/1

9 781722 506285